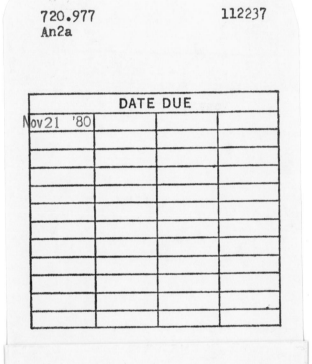

| DATE DUE | | | |
|---|---|---|---|
| Nov21 '80 | | | |
| | | | |
| | | | |
| | | | |
| | | | |
| | | | |
| | | | |
| | | | |
| | | | |
| | | | |
| | | | |

# BOOKS BY WAYNE ANDREWS

*Architecture in New England*

*Siegfried's Curse: The German Journey from Nietzsche to Hesse*

*Architecture in New York*

*Architecture in Chicago and Mid-America*

*Architecture in Michigan*

*Germaine: A Portrait of Madame De Staël*

*Architecture in America*

*Architecture, Ambition and Americans*

*Who Has Been Tampering with These Pianos?*
   *(under the pseudonym Montagu O'Reilly)*

*Battle for Chicago*

*The Vanderbilt Legend*

# ARCHITECTURE IN CHICAGO AND MID-AMERICA

# ARCHITECTURE IN CHICAGO & MID-AMERICA

## A PHOTOGRAPHIC HISTORY

# WAYNE ANDREWS

Icon Editions
Harper & Row, Publishers
New York, Evanston, San Francisco, London

FOR MY FATHER, EMORY COBB ANDREWS

*First Icon Edition published 1973.*

# PHOTOGRAPHIC CREDITS AND ACKNOWLEDGMENTS

I am indebted to Richard Nickel, 1508 Grove Avenue, Park Ridge, Ill., for his photographs of the interior of the Schiller Building (49), the Wainwright Building (51) and the entrance to the Chicago Stock Exchange (53); to Leco Photo Service, 1 East 42nd Street, New York City, and to R. Buckminster Fuller for the photographs of the Climatron (176) and the exterior and interior of the Fuller house at Carbondale (177); to Hedrich Blessing, 450 East Ontario Street, Chicago, for the photograph of the lakefront reproduced in the introduction and for photographs of the Federal Center (168), the Farnsworth house (169) and the Inland Steel Building (170); to the Chicago Historical Society for the photographs of the exterior and interior of the Palmer House (21), the Marshall Field residence (22), the MacVeagh residence (24), the Administration Building (61), the Agricultural and the Manufactures Buildings (62), the Fisheries Building (63), and the Transportation Building (64); to the Chicago Architectural Photographing Co., 75 East Wacker Drive, Chicago, for photographs of the Marshall Field warehouse (23), the Potter Palmer castle (29), the Home Insurance Building (36), the Tacoma Building (38), the Monadnock Building (40), the Woman's Temple (41), the Masonic Temple (42), the Schiller Building (48), the exterior and interior of the Avery Coonley residence (78 and 79), the Midway Gardens (81) and the Chapin & Gore Building (86).

All other photographs are my own.

But I owe the greatest debt of all to Richard Schuler, Ernest Pile, Sybil Collins and the other members of the staff of Compo Photo Service, 220 West 42nd Street, New York, who have so carefully developed and enlarged my negatives and given me the benefit of their experience. This book would have been impossible without their complete co-operation.

The quotations from Louis Sullivan's *Autobiography of an Idea* are reproduced by courtesy of the American Institute of Architects.

Many architects have been helpful, especially Barry Byrne, the late George Grant Elmslie, the late Mrs. Walter Burley Griffin (Marion Mahony), the late William Gray Purcell, and Benjamin and Harry Weese. Aline Saarinen was so kind as to arrange a meeting with Eero Saarinen.

And many other people have been enlightening. Leonard K. Eaton discussed his forthcoming book on the clients of Wright and Shaw. W. Hawkins Ferry, author of the forthcoming *Buildings of Detroit* (Wayne University Press, 1968), answered innumerable questions about the architecture of Michigan. Mrs. Sidney Haskins helped me explore the work of her father, Howard Van Doren Shaw. Roger G. Kennedy gave me priceless advice on the subject of Harvey Ellis. Mrs. Paul M. Rhymner of the Chicago Historical Society saved me an immense amount of time while I was checking the Society's picture files. E. P. Richardson discovered for me the Allen house in Des Moines. Dimitri Tselos generously let me read his forthcoming article on the World's Fair of 1893 for the *Journal of the Society of Architectural Historians*, and Thomas C. Cochran was so obliging as to read the introduction.

Finally, Mr. and Mrs. Harwell Hamilton Harris have been more than enlightening.

# INTRODUCTION: CHICAGO IS WHERE IT HAPPENED

Chicago has always meant all things to all men.

To Mrs. Astor's great and good friend Ward McAllister, America's second city was capable of infinite improvement. "The contact of New York and Chicago society cannot help but open the eyes of our Western natives to our superiority," he explained on the eve of the World's Fair of 1893. "I do not wish to belittle Chicago in using the word *superiority*. The society of Chicago is behind that of New York, but there is no reason why it should not eventually catch up. Chicago is moving in the right direction and should be encouraged in every way."

On the other hand, the packer Gustavus Franklin Swift thought Chicago was good enough as it was. Here, he implored a reporter to remember, "is the finest city in the world for the moderate, natural, average man of affairs in which to live. The New Yorker who says Chicago is a city of no luxuries is probably one of that constantly growing number who are insatiable in their greed for the softer things of life. To those men who have families and who find in their homes the greatest of their pleasures, Chicago offers all that New York offers, and in my opinion more. A man can get wholesome food in Chicago more cheaply than he can in the East, and he can live as well on a smaller amount of money. I do not go in for luxuries myself."

So much for the verdict of McAllister and Swift. To architects and to that apparently growing number of people who find architecture a fascinating subject, *Chicago is where it happened*. They know that Chicago can claim, as can no other city, to be the birthplace of modern architecture.

Ambition was in the air as early as 1883, when William Le Baron Jenney, an engineer lately on the staffs of Sherman and Grant, invented the eleven-story Home Insurance Building for the southwest corner of LaSalle and Adams Streets. This is gener-ally considered to be the world's first skyscraper: that is, the world's first tall steel-frame building. To be technical for a moment, wrought iron formed the skeleton up to and including the sixth story; beyond that point Bessemer steel beams were used. Whether or not the skeleton in this instance did *all* the work of the walls has been debated; there are those who insist that the honor of being the world's first must be assigned the Tacoma Building, con-ceived three years later for the northeast corner of LaSalle and Madison by the firm of Holabird & Roche. Whichever way you have it, Chicagoans were the first to prove that walls were no longer needed to perform the ancient function of support. Hereafter walls could be thin as silk, as Viollet-le-Duc had been arguing in France from his studies of the engineering of the Gothic cathedrals.

What began with the Home Insurance and Ta-coma Buildings could not be arrested. Daniel Hud-son Burnham and John Wellborn Root, greater art-ists by far than the gentlemen just mentioned, worked their sure will on tall buildings, and by 1889 the firm of Adler & Sullivan completed the incom-parable Auditorium, a hotel combined with an opera house of unimpeachable acoustics. Out of the Adler & Sullivan office came Frank Lloyd Wright, who shattered in his twenties the useless conven-tions governing the design of the American home. "Democracy," cried Wright, "needed something basically better than the box." Chicago began set-ting the standards and Chicago architects began in-vading not only Saint Louis and the Twin Cities but the entire Middle West. This marvelous momentum came to a temporary halt in the 1920s, but Eliel Saarinen, who did his best to redeem the decade by his work at Cranbrook near Detroit, might never have left Finland for America if he had not won second prize in the contest for Chicago's Tribune Tower. And his son Eero Saarinen might never have arrived at the lethal accuracy of the General Motors Technical Center at Warren, Michigan—the most distinguished monument yet erected to the glory of a giant corporation—if he had not watched Ludwig Miës van der Rohe, the German who settled in Chicago in 1938, at work on the campus of the Illinois Institute of Technology. As for Albert Kahn, the Detroiter who became the master designer of factories, he too was Chicago-inspired when he laid out the General Motors Building in Detroit, which owes so much to the classical message of Burnham's last skyscrapers.

This is not the same thing as saying that Chicago either was or is paradise on earth. In the late nineteenth and early twentieth centuries it was a haunted city, as romantic or impractical in its way as the Old South. From which you must not infer that wisteria takes kindly to the soil of Illinois. Chicago lived in the shadow of its great millionaires, whose pronouncements on every subject were accorded the reverence the South granted the dying words of Stonewall Jackson.

Now that the millionaires have been brought back to mind, this may be the moment to listen to the singular complaint of the Chicago novelist Henry B. Fuller. "This town of ours," he decided back in 1895, "labors under one peculiar disadvantage: it is the only great city in the world to which all of its citizens have come for the one common, avowed object of making money. There you have its genesis, its growth, its end and object; and there are very few of us who are not attending to that object very strictly. In this Garden City of ours every man cultivates his own little bed and his neighbor his; but who looks after the paths between?"

Fuller did not need to be told that leisure in Chicago was usually regarded as an invitation to sin. Erastus Brainerd, the banker in his novel *The Cliff-Dwellers*, "had never lived for anything but business. . . . He never dreamed of anything but business—he had never worn a dress-coat in his life. He wrote about nothing but business—his nearest relative was never more than 'dear sir' and he himself was never more than 'yours truly'; and he wrote on business letterheads even to his own family."

In Chicago life was earnest, no doubt of that. Wit and grace could not be easily commanded. It is true that Julia Loomis Newberry, whose father's fortune built the Newberry Library, might have brought the touch of Jane Austen to bear on the North Side, but she did not live to write the novels for which she was so exquisitely prepared. When barely twenty-two she died of tuberculosis in Rome, leaving merely her diary, in which at fifteen she proclaimed that her father's New York friend Stuyvesant Fish "in spite of his having a grandfather" was "little less than an idiot."

Wit and grace may be ingredients without which no literary or artistic center can exist, but architects, as the history of Chicago triumphantly proves, can not only survive but thrive in a serious-minded environment. The strange charm of Chicago, recalling in an oblique way that of the South, may be said to reside in the conflict between the strenuous ideals of the great businessmen and the demands of everyday life. The South could not live, and it has not lived, on the capital bequeathed by Robert E. Lee: a superb manner is not necessarily an asset in running a grocery store. Nor could Chicago *quite* conform to the commandments of Swift, Armour and Field: the very attempt would have been inhuman.

Except for Cyrus Hall McCormick, a sturdy Scotch-Irish immigrant from the Back Parts of Virginia, the great Chicago millionaires seem to have come from small towns in New England or from those regions of New York State overrun by New Englanders. The East they remembered was not Boston or Concord but some hamlet where the reading of Ralph Waldo Emerson was confined to the quarters of an eccentric schoolmaster.

Philip Danforth Armour, a native of Stockbridge, Madison County, New York, might be considered typical, if that be any way to describe the businessman who came closer than anyone else to being the folk hero of the city. "My culture is mostly in my wife's name," he confided to Elbert Hubbard, who did not hesitate to report that the packer's vocabulary "needed to be put on a buffing wheel. His stories often required formaldehyde."

"You have made your pile; why not clear out?" Armour was one day asked by a reporter. "I have no other interest in life but my business," came the answer. "I do not want any more money; as you say, I have more than I want. I do not love the money. What I do love is the getting of it. All these years of my life I have put into this work, and now it is my life and I cannot give it up. What other interest can you suggest to me? I do not read. I do not take any part in politics. What can I do? Besides, I think it is well for me to remain in business to set an example to the younger men who are coming up around me."

He did set an example. He liked to get down to work "before the boys with the polished nails show up," which meant that he got to the office at seven. He stayed there until six in the evening, occasionally staring stubbornly at the bunch of fresh flowers his secretary stuck in the ox-horn vase on his desk. At nine o'clock, having had a wholesome dinner in his own home on Prairie Avenue, he went straight to bed. There was nothing eccentric about his habits, and policemen were accustomed to set their watches by his coming and going.

"When I am done with work," he told a favorite employee, "remember this—that I always had a great respect for facts. If there were fewer theorists in the world, there would be more successes. Facts can be discounted in any bank, but a theory is rarely worth par. Stick to facts." He had grown up near the socialist community of Oneida but had never been tempted by the ideology of John Humphrey Noyes. "Oneida is for those whose dream did not come true," he chortled. "Mine has."

But there was one unpleasant fact that Armour was obliged to face, and that was the presence, nearby on Prairie Avenue, of Marshall Field. The master of the great department store did not leave home until nine in the morning, and invariably closed his desk at four in the afternoon. "I have never believed in overworking, either as applied to myself or others," he made plain. "It is paid for with a short life, and I do not believe in it."

The hours that Field kept were a constant mortification to Armour. "It must be wonderful to have a business like yours . . . and keep banker's hours," the packer rebuked the merchant prince when they were aboard a private car on an inspection trip of the Chicago, St. Paul & Milwaukee Railroad. On this very trip Field made the mistake of proposing a game of cards at nine in the evening. "I have not broken my retiring hour for Mrs. Armour," came the quick rebuff, "and I see no reason to do it for you."

Field was a cool man, but Chicago listened, quite correctly, to what he had to say. When he died in the winter of 1906 he left an estate of $120,000,000, twelve times bigger than that of Cyrus Hall McCormick, ten times bigger than that of Swift, and four times bigger than that of Armour himself.

Field had always known there was a gray charm to saving money. "As a rule," he told—of all people —Theodore Dreiser, "people do not know how to save. The average young man of today, when he begins to earn is soon inclined to habits of extravagance and wastefulness; gets somehow imbued with the idea that irrespective of what he earns, he must indulge in habits corresponding to those of some other young man, simply because he imagines that he cannot be manly without. The five, ten or fifteen cents a day that is squandered, while a mere trifle apparently, if saved would in a few years amount to thousands of dollars and go far toward establishing a future career." It was evident that he agreed with Swift that "no young man is rich enough to smoke twenty-five-cent cigars."

As for a college education, it was at best a questionable investment. "The truth is," Field enlightened Dreiser, "that for most young men a college education means that just at the time when they should be having business principles instilled into them, and be getting themselves energetically pulled together for their life's work, they are sent to college. Then intervenes what many a young man looks back on as the jolliest time of his life. . . . Often when he comes out of college this young man is unfitted by this good time to buckle down to hard work, and the result is a failure to grasp opportunities that would have opened the way for a successful career."

So much for the philosophy of the lords of Chicago. The time has come to announce the arrival in the city, on the day before Thanksgiving, 1873, of Louis Henri Sullivan, one of the great architects of the last hundred years. Sullivan lived all his life in a world far removed from that of Armour, Swift and Field. Indeed, too far removed, for the Chicago in which he believed was a city in the clouds.

In his autobiography Sullivan maintained that "the beauty, the passion, the glory of the past shall merge into a new beauty, a new passion, a new glory as man approaches man, and recognizing him, rejoices in him, and with him, as born in power." He also claimed that "never . . . has there been such sound warrant for an attitude of optimism." This does come strangely from a man who lived through the Haymarket Riot and the Pullman Strike and witnessed the campaign to defame Governor Altgeld for doing something sensible and humane in such emergencies.

Sullivan was a muddled thinker. His writings are often embarrassing. He read—or misread—volume after volume of Emerson, Herbert Spencer, Nietzsche and Veblen, and the half-digested ideas of these men reappear with alarming frequency in his vague prose. But Sullivan was after all an architect, not a writer. Although Stanford White and Augustus Saint-Gaudens could come dangerously close—as in the clock on the stairs of the Villard house in New York—to his skill as a decorator, no one has surpassed him as a designer of skyscrapers. The Guaranty Building in Buffalo and the Wainwright Building in Saint Louis remain to reprove the attempts of later generations to cope with the essence of the tall steel frame. Furthermore, he and his partner Dankmar Adler created the Auditorium.

The Auditorium has been mentioned for the second time, and not just because I should like to point out that my father, a perfect Wagnerite if ever there was one, was anxious to carry a spear in every performance he could manage of the master's works. The Auditorium has been given this emphasis because it contains—there is no point in being shy about the matter—the greatest opera house in the world in every respect: here Chicago surpasses even Paris. Its stage was dark for many years, but this was not the fault of Sullivan, but of Samuel Insull, who insisted on building a new opera house in 1929, an immense pile on the banks of the Chicago River, designed by Graham, Anderson, Probst

& White, the somewhat uninspired successors of D. H. Burnham. However, the Auditorium has now been restored, and reverently, by Harry M. Weese & Associates, and on October 31, 1967, it was reopened with the New York City Ballet's production of *A Midsummer Night's Dream.* Long before this, the hotel end of the Auditorium was given over, thanks to the generosity of the late Marshall Field III and the Julius Rosenwald Fund, to Roosevelt University.

The chief designer of this masterpiece was born in 1856 in Boston. But you must not imagine that his ties to New England were strong, or that he enjoyed as a little boy any of the security an insider had the right to demand. He was definitely an outsider. His father was a dancing-master from Ireland; his mother, a pianist from Geneva, was half Swiss-French, half German. Apparently the only strong character of Sullivan's childhood was his maternal grandfather, who took him on walks at night to contemplate the stars.

Too much has not been said about Sullivan's early years, for he remained, all his life, a prisoner of his childhood, to which two thirds of his autobiography are surrendered. His childhood came to an end the day he entered the architectural school at M.I.T., where he studied under Professor William R. Ware. To Sullivan he was no paragon; we are even told that he was "not imaginative enough to be ardent." Which may not be quite fair to this professor. He was devoted to Ruskin, as were nearly all the men who made their mark in the early annals of modern architecture. He was also the partner of Henry Van Brunt, who took the trouble to translate into English the famous *Discourses on Architecture* of Viollet-le-Duc. For Sullivan, as for Frank Lloyd Wright, Viollet-le-Duc spoke with the authority of a prophet.

Quitting M.I.T. at the end of his first year, Sullivan went on to New York, where he had a good hour or two with Richard Morris Hunt on the advantages of studying at the Ecole des Beaux Arts, and then to Philadelphia, where he talked himself into a job as a draftsman with the firm of Furness & Hewitt, doggedly committed, both partners, to the gospel of Ruskin. The Depression of 1873 put an end to his career in Philadelphia and sent him on to Chicago, where he discovered "an energy that made him tingle to be in the game." There he met William Le Baron Jenney and the rest of the crew who were to fashion the first skyscrapers.

By the summer of 1874 he was off to France, where he entered the atelier of one Emile Vaudremer at the Ecole. This experience seems to have done him no harm, in spite of the legend, still to be heard in stuffy classrooms, that the teaching at the Ecole was horridly academic. It was in Paris that he came across a tutor in mathematics by the name of Clopet who was proud of advancing demonstrations so broad as to admit of no exception. Sullivan, who was never famous for his sense of humor, was struck, fatally, by this notion. "If this can be done in mathematics, why not in architecture?" he recorded in his autobiography. "The instant answer: It can, and it shall be! *No one has*—I will!" Here no doubt was the germ of the oversimplification *Form follows function* for which Sullivan will unfortunately be remembered. In his architecture he was never dogmatic. Yet he was to strike again and again the stiff attitudes of a schoolmaster whose students have not completed their assignments. "The Master's very walk bore a dangerous resemblance to a strut," Frank Lloyd Wright has told us.

Back in Chicago, on the first of May, 1881, Sullivan became the partner of Dankmar Adler. Twelve years older than he, Adler was the rock he desperately needed. Born in Germany, the son of a rabbi who moved first to Detroit and then to Chicago, he was a formidable authority on acoustics—Carnegie Hall in New York City owes its acoustical supremacy to his advice—and a remarkable engineer. He was, Wright remembered, "one to inspire others with confidence in his power at once."

The partners could not overlook the completion in 1887 of Marshall Field's wholesale store or warehouse. The work of Henry Hobson Richardson—who brought order out of the chaos that followed the Civil War, planning Trinity Church in Boston, whose simplified massing and imperial command of granite set a standard to which architects rallied from coast to coast—the Field warehouse was the model of dignity in downtown Chicago. The lesson was not lost on Adler & Sullivan when they began their Auditorium. Scrapping their first ambiguous elevations, they brought a new simplicity to Michigan Boulevard. In the opera house itself Sullivan spent his magnificent decorative gift on the vast elliptical arches and the golden frame for the stage. When these splendors were opened to the public on the ninth of December, 1889, and Adelina Patti rendered "Home, Sweet Home" before an audience that included the Marshall Fields and the George M. Pullmans, even President Harrison, who was not exactly renowned for his appreciation of the fine arts, was impressed. "New York surrenders, eh?" Harrison commented as he nudged the shoulder of Vice-President Levi P. Morton from the Empire State.

With such a success for the Adler & Sullivan office, the younger partner could look with equanimity at the work of his competitors. He had, however, to respect the work of Burnham & Root, who were responsible for the Richardsonian grandeurs of the Rookery, the Woman's Temple and the Masonic Temple, three of the unforgettable skyscrapers, and for the Monadnock Building. This last, which made use of masonry bearing walls rather than the steel-frame method of construction, was alleged to be the work of Root alone. It was bare of all ornament, a monument to the investment in Chicago real estate of the trustees of the fortune of Henry Adams' grandfather, Peter Chardon Brooks of Boston.

"My idea," Burnham said to Sullivan, "is to work up a big big business, to handle big things, deal with big businessmen, and to build up a big organization, for you can't handle big things unless you have an organization." Sullivan had now met the man who was qualified as was no one else to face Chicago head on. "He was elephantine, tactless and blurting," the designer of the Auditorium recalled. "He got many a humiliating knock on the nose in his quest of the big; but he faltered not—his purpose was fixed. Himself not especially susceptible to flattery except in a sentimental way, he soon learned its efficacy when plastered thick on big businessmen." But this was also the man who turned to Sullivan one evening and said: "See! Louis, how beautiful the moon is now, overhead, how tender. Something in her beauty suggests tears to me."

As for Root, he too was a personality. "He was not of Burnham's type," Sullivan reported, "but . . . a man of quick-witted all-around culture which he carried easily and jauntily, and vain to the limit of the skies. . . . His temperament was that of the well-groomed free-lance, never taking anything too seriously, wherein he differed from his ponderous partner, much as dragon-fly and mastiff. Nor had he one tenth of his partner's settled will, nor of said partner's capacity to go through hell to reach an end. John Root's immediate ambition was to shine."

In the meantime, enterprising Chicagoans were descending on Washington to plead the city's right to be the site of a World's Fair honoring the 400th anniversary of the discovery of America, and the day came when the House of Representatives agreed. The buildings were to be dedicated in 1892, and the Fair itself to open for six months beginning May 1, 1893. To Root this was Chicago's chance to rival the recent expositions in Paris. "We have more space, more money, and we have the lake," he commented. "Why should we not surpass Paris?" He died of pneumonia early in 1891 while the Fair was still in the early stages, but had already reported to the Committee on Grounds and Buildings that "it would be wise to select a certain number of architects because of their prominence in the profession, choosing each man for such work as would be most parallel with his best achievements." What this meant was that Burnham & Root, as administrators, would design no buildings themselves for the Fair, and that Chicago would be informed by the last word from the East.

A revolution, no less, had recently taken place in New York, where in 1881 Richard Morris Hunt hit on the happy idea of building a palace in Caen limestone in the manner of the early French Renaissance for Mr. and Mrs. W. K. Vanderbilt. After years of searching, Hunt had arrived at the perfect formula for a millionaire's town house: his success was made more than evident when the Vanderbilts humbled the Astors on the evening of March 26, 1883, by giving in their new and noble château the

grandest party in the history of Manhattan Island.

This rediscovery of the Renaissance and its charms could not be ignored by Hunt's rivals. Suddenly the firm of McKim, Mead & White, who had gone a long way on the road to modern architecture in the informal shingle-style houses they had been contriving for Newport and other summer resorts, made an about-face. The complex of five adjoining houses they created in 1885 for the railroad magnate Henry Villard and four of his friends—still standing, these houses, to the rear of St. Patrick's Cathedral—indicated that they would be henceforth as dedicated to the ideals of the Renaissance as Hunt himself. That strange thing called taste had changed. The change was almost immediately noted in Chicago, where Hunt in 1884 provided a château very like that of the W. K. Vanderbilts for the William Bordens. The Bordens could not be said to draw upon the unlimited resources of the Vanderbilts, but William's father had recently amassed something like $2,300,000 by joining Marshall Field in buying up a silver mine or two at Leadville, Colorado.

There was no public protest when the Bordens moved into their new house on Lake Shore Drive, and you might suppose that there would be no protest over inviting Richard Morris Hunt, McKim, Mead & White and a few other distinguished firms from the East to contribute to the Fair. A protest, however, was made, and the fiercest controversy in the history of American architecture is still raging over the lagoons that graced Jackson Park in the summer of 1893.

The reasons for the controversy, ancient though it may be, are worth looking into. First of all, the Fair was a tremendous success. Four hundred thousand people poured through the turnstiles on the opening day, and Ward McAllister showed a genuine concern over the hearty hospitality promised Easterners by Mayor Carter H. Harrison. "I may say," McAllister announced, "that it is not quantity but quality that society people want. Hospitality which includes the whole human race is not desirable."

Secondly, a number of foolish statements about the Fair were made by men who should have known better. The sculptor Saint-Gaudens, for example, revealed that he was a member in good standing of what must be called a mutual-admiration society. "Look here, old fellow," he called out at the end of a conference attended by Hunt and McKim, "do you realize that this is the greatest meeting of artists since the fifteenth century?" And it must be admitted that Burnham was a trifle too apologetic when face to face with the great men of the East: his name cannot be dropped from the list of those who have made their contribution to the history of Chicago's famous inferiority complex. "We have been in an inventive period, and have had rather a contempt for the classics," he suggested. "Men evolved new ideas and imagined they could start a new school without much reference to the past." A little of this sort of thing went a long way with Hunt, who was certain to explode at the slightest hint of the cultural inferiority of the city in which he found himself. "Hell," he broke into one of Burnham's discourses, "we haven't come out here on a missionary expedition. Let's get down to work."

By now we have nearly everything that was needed to start the controversy over the Fair. Things were going very well indeed, so well that a little resentment would be natural, particularly on the part of those who realized that Saint-Gaudens could be pompous at times, and sensed that Burnham had sold Chicago short in running down his own early work. For tempers to snap, there was only one thing missing, and it was not missing for long. This was the entrance upon the scene of those curious people (some of them are still with us today) who believed that modern architecture was a tender flower, very like an orchid, which might fade away if set in the shade of a building in the Renaissance manner.

It is interesting that Sullivan does not seem to have belonged to this group in 1893. He had, of course, no reason to. He was not slighted, not in the least. He and Henry Ives Cobb (whose Fisheries Building was a thing in the Richardsonian style) had been selected to represent the Chicago point of view. Moreover, Sullivan's Transportation Building, the salient feature of which was a gorgeously decorated golden doorway, was, in the opinion of many people, the outstanding exhibit of the art of architecture at the Fair. In any event, he was the only architect to be recognized in Europe: in the next year he received three medals from the Union Centrale des Arts Décoratifs.

As for the exhibits of Hunt and of McKim, Mead & White, neither the former's Administration Building nor the latter's Agricultural Building added a single leaf to their laurels. Better things had been done before by Hunt and McKim, Mead & White; better things would be done in the future. While it is true that the sight of these classic façades sent Henry Adams into ecstasy, he seems to have been less excited by their beauty than by the claims that might now be advanced for the social position of artists and intellectuals in the United States. "Chicago," he said, referring to the Fair, "was the first expression of American thought as a unity." This was bunk. "If," he went on, "the people of the Northwest actually knew what was good when they saw it, they would some day talk about Hunt and Richardson, La Farge and Saint-Gaudens, Burnham and McKim and Stanford White, when their politicians and millionaires were otherwise forgotten."

A shrewder estimate of the Fair as a whole was made by the leading architectural critic of the day, Montgomery Schuyler. "Arcadian architecture is one thing and American architecture another," he declared. "Men bring not back the mastodons nor we those times."

But to return to Sullivan. The business of Adler & Sullivan, like that of many other firms, declined in the wake of the depression of 1893, and on the eleventh of July, 1895, Adler decided he must retire from the practice of architecture to become consulting architect and general sales manager of the Crane Elevator Company. For Sullivan this was a blow from which he never recovered. His genius, of course, was never to fail him, but without Adler's business sense to guide him, he was a lost man. On his own (with the assistance of his faithful associate George Elmslie) he was to design the marvelously ornamented department store of Schlesinger & Mayer, now occupied by Carson, Pirie Scott & Co., and he even ventured into New York City, where he and Lyndon P. Smith created the now battered and abused Bayard Building on Bleecker Street. But he seems to have lost the touch that attracted the big clients. In the end he was reduced to planning banks for country towns in the Middle West. These were often works of art. The best of them all, the National Farmers Bank at Owatonna, Minnesota, which he and Elmslie completed in 1908, has recently been restored and enlarged with the utmost sympathy by Harwell Hamilton Harris.

On the fourteenth of April, 1924, he died of neuritis, complicated by an overuse of stimulants, in a mediocre South Side hotel. He had been a drunk for years, he was a beaten man, and it will always be accounted a tragedy that the twentieth century made such thin use of his talents.

It was in the year of his death that he published *The Autobiography of an Idea*. When he at last came to write his reminiscences it dawned upon him that the World's Fair of 1893 should bear the responsibility for bringing about his ruin. He turned pale at the thought of the crowds that had pushed through the turnstiles in that far-off summer:

*"These crowds were astonished. They beheld what was for them an amazing revelation of the architectural art, of which previously they in comparison had known nothing. . . . They departed joyously, carriers of contagion, unaware that what they had beheld and believed to be truth was to prove, in historic fact, an appalling calamity. For what they saw was not what they believed they saw, but an imposition of the spurious upon their eyesight, a naked exhibitionism of charlatanry in the higher feudal and dominating culture, conjoined with expert salesmanship in the materials of decay. . . .*

*"The damage wrought by the World's Fair will last for half a century from its date, if not longer. It has penetrated deep into the constitution of the American mind, effecting there lesions significant of dementia."*

Once these paragraphs are stripped of their rhetoric, it will be evident that Sullivan aimed to erase a great many sites from the map of the United States. His abomination of the Renaissance had become an obsession. If the Fair was as bad as he believed, any expression of the Renaissance spirit was an indecency—whether the colonial monuments of Charleston, the palaces of Newport, or the capitol at Washington. A calmer man might have recognized that there was a place for both modern and un-modern architecture. This is the position taken by many a modern architect in 1968, when Maybeck's classical Palace of Fine Arts by the Golden Gate is deeply admired and McKim's classical Pennsylvania Station in New York is sorely missed.

As for the damage done by the Fair, it was exaggerated. Although Sullivan had next to no work in the twenty-five years following 1893, this was the very period in which the members of the Chicago School, all of whom may be said to have followed in his footsteps, won a considerable reputation. This is not the place to list all the members of the Chicago School, minor or major, but they have their importance, even if they have not yet become household names—as you can find out for yourself if you make light of the accomplishments of Walter Burley Griffin or Purcell & Elmslie in the presence of an architectural historian.

Finally, it was in the twenty-five years following 1893 that Frank Lloyd Wright conquered Chicago and incidentally the world.

It is true that Wright enjoyed one advantage beyond Sullivan's reach. The Welsh clan from which he sprang in Wisconsin was a tower of strength long before he built Taliesin at Spring Green. Wright's father may have been a failure, but he had once been a preacher in New England and was even a distant relative of James Russell Lowell. This was capital upon which Wright could always draw in a Middle West so easily awed by the East. As for Wright's mother, she had a will of iron, and he could always speak with the confidence of one who came from a family that would not be ignored.

There is no time and there certainly is no need to tell the details of Wright's career. Everyone has heard of his apprenticeship in the office of Adler & Sullivan, and nearly everyone knows that in the summer of 1893, having been caught designing private houses for his own account on the firm's time, he was fired. "If Wright were honest," Sullivan later told George Elmslie, "he'd be half a man." There is a temptation to pause over this incident, for Sullivan had no interest in domestic architecture, and if his chief draftsman had stayed by him, his troubles might never have descended. What may be more significant, however, is Wright's description of the post he held under his *lieber Meister*. He was not the *best* draftsman, no. He was the *best-paid draftsman in the city of Chicago*. Here was a man that P. D. Armour would have had to respect.

"You've got to have guts to be an architect!" Wright kept insisting. "People will come to you and tell you what they want, and you will have to give them what they need." Here was a man who could capture the admiration of D. H. Burnham. He did. The older man, so we are informed by Wright's autobiography, was so kind as to offer him four years at the Ecole des Beaux Arts and in addition two years at the Academy in Rome, with all expenses paid and his family supported in the meantime. At the end of these years abroad he was to step into a sure job with D. H. Burnham & Co.

Wright has written that he refused this great opportunity. "No, Mr. Burnham. . . . I can't run away from what I see as mine."

What Burnham must have seen was that Wright had already digested the Renaissance. This will seem very odd to those who have read Wright's works more carefully than they have examined his buildings. He was guilty of a number of strange pronouncements on this subject; he even claimed one day that the Renaissance "was not a development . . . it was a disease." If indeed it was a disease, no one was more thoroughly exposed than the young man who turned down the chance to study in Paris and Rome. While still in Sullivan's office he planned a quite competent colonial-revival house for George Blossom on the South Side, proving that he was willing, at least on this occasion, to experiment with the Renaissance as reflected in colonial and federal New England. And if, as may be argued, the message of the Italian masters from Bramante to Palladio was that of uncanny symmetry and harmony, he was in need of no instruction whatever, as a glance at the Willitts house of 1902 will indicate.

Perhaps the time has come to recognize that

Wright not only learned much from the Renaissance but also owed more to D. H. Burnham than he has told us. Burnham could have taught him the art of survival, which has always been a useful art for an architect to master. It is true that Sullivan might have sympathized, as Burnham could not, with the doctrines he was to make world-famous—the necessity of expressing the nature of materials, the use and never the abuse of a site, and the breaking down of the partitions that constricted the flow of interior space. But Burnham, and Burnham alone, could have grasped the ambition that was to carry the lord of Taliesin through the timid 1920s down to the goals of his last years.

"Early in life," said Wright, "I had to choose between honest arrogance and hypocritical humility. I chose honest arrogance and have seen no reason to change." A certain doubt exists as to when or where this conception occurred to the master, but it is likely the site of the inspiration was the Chicago lakefront, Burnham's very own creation.

"Make no little plans," Burnham urged the Commercial Club in 1909, when the present glory of Michigan Avenue, Lake Shore Drive and the various outer drives was a thing far in the future. "They have no magic to stir men's blood and probably themselves will not be realized. Make big plans; aim high in hope and work, remembering that a noble, logical diagram will never die, but long after we are gone will be a living thing, asserting itself with ever-growing insistency. Remember that our sons and grandsons are going to do things that would stagger us. Let your watchword be order and your beacon beauty."

The Chicago Plan, which makes the lakefront the most spectacular man-made site in the western hemisphere, might never have been conceived, it seems fairly obvious, if Burnham had not been so intimately concerned in the summer of 1893 with the layout of the buildings on the lake's edge and in Jackson Park. Out of the World's Fair also came Burnham's predilection for the classical revival, handsomely represented on Michigan Avenue by his Railway Exchange and People's Gas Building. These imposing structures offer no evidence of a criminal intent on the part of the designer, even though he could never hope to be as subtle as Louis Sullivan.

Who knows, such a thought may even have come to Frank Lloyd Wright early in his career on his way home to Oak Park. He was always a man of uncommon sense, and was never shrewder than when he settled in the suburb Ernest Hemingway was to run away from. The affluence of the North Shore, where temperatures, thanks to the lake, range from ten to fifteen degrees cooler on summer days, was not Wright's to command. But in the more modest surroundings of Oak Park the commandments of Armour, Swift and Field might be less distinctly heard. Life in a western suburb might be less expensive than in Winnetka or Lake Forest. It could also be less orthodox.

This is not to say that Wright fled for a second the tension that was ever in the air of Chicago.

Tensions may intimidate weak artists but strengthen the strong, as Friedrich Nietzsche understood when he wrote that "art alone is what keeps the bow from snapping."

It may be too soon in 1968 to measure what has been determined, dared and done since the deaths of Eliel and Eero Saarinen and Frank Lloyd Wright, but it is obvious that the Middle West continues to be an attractive terrain to architects answering questions that have not yet been asked. No one can predict, for example, what surprises a firm like Meathe, Kessler & Associates may have planned for tomorrow.

In any event, it is a happy fact and not a boast that in the last hundred years no nation in the world has matched the architecture of Chicago and the Middle West.

*In Memoriam D. H. Burnham: The lakefront in the summer of 1967.*

# CONTENTS

*Capital from the Mormon Temple at Nauvoo, Illinois, 1841–46 (architect unknown). Elder William Weeks was retained as "architect," but whether he was more than a draftsman who took orders from Joseph Smith remains to be proved. Arsonists burned the temple to the ground in 1848; a mate to this capital from Nauvoo may be seen on the grounds of the Historical Society at Quincy. The prophet Joseph Smith and his brother Hyrum were murdered by the mob that assailed the jail at Carthage, Illinois, on June 27, 1844.*

The Middle West has yet to apply for the copyright on conformity. There have always been pockets of resistance to prevailing opinions. The Mormons provided an early example. So did the founders of the utopian communities of New Harmony, Bishop Hill and Zoar.

*Mormon Temple, Kirtland, Ohio, 1833–36 (architect unknown). The Mormons tarried in Ohio before descending on Commerce, Illinois, and renaming it Nauvoo.*

*Two views of the residence of David Dale Owen, New Harmony, Indiana, 1859 (David Dale Owen and James Renwick, Jr.). New Harmony was first settled by George Rapp and his fellow pietists, who fled Württemberg to establish a religious community in the New World free from the threat of official dogmatism. In 1825 the lands were sold to Robert Owen, the British mill-owner, who saw here the chance to build a socialist utopia. His son David Dale Owen, a geologist who was the first to emphasize the mineral resources of Iowa and Wisconsin, called on Renwick, the architect of Grace Church, New York, for assistance in designing this Gothic Revival dwelling. Robert Dale Owen, David's brother, publicized Renwick's plan for the Smithsonian Institution in Washington.*

3

*Roofless Church, New Harmony, Indiana, 1960 (Philip C. Johnson). Complete with a sculpture by Jacques Lipchitz, this church was erected in memory of the sacrifices of the Rappites and Owenites.*

OPPOSITE ABOVE: *Steeple Building, Bishop Hill, Illinois, 1854 (architect unknown).* BELOW: *Communal housing, Bishop Hill, Illinois, 1854 (architect unknown). Bishop Hill was the creation of Swedish pietists led by Olaf Olson.*

*Number One House, Zoar, Ohio, 1835 (architect unknown). Zoar was built by the followers of Joseph Bäumeler, a German separatist who brought his colony to America in 1817. Number One House, recalling the architecture of the eighteenth century on the Eastern Seaboard, was originally intended to house the aged. It became Bäumeler's own headquarters.*

The romantic years—from 1830 to 1860—witnessed in the Middle West as else-where in America the expansion of the Greek and Gothic Revivals, both of which had been introduced in 1799 to Philadelphia by Benjamin Henry Latrobe, chief architect of the Capitol in Washington.

*Residence of Dr. Andrew L. Hays, Marshall, Michigan, c. 1838 (architect un-known). This may be the finest Greek Revival mansion in Michigan.*

ABOVE: *The Elms, Hudson, Ohio, 1850–53 (Simeon Porter?).*

BELOW: *Honolulu House, residence of Abner Platt, Marshall, Michigan, 1860 (architect unknown). The Elms gives some indication of the range of Gothic fantasy in the Middle West. Platt's bracketed Italian villa, following yet another popular style in the romantic years, may have been inspired by the work of Henry Austin around New Haven, Connecticut. Platt had been consul in the Hawaiian Islands.*

*Hillforest, residence of Thomas Gaff, Aurora, Indiana, 1852–56 (architect unknown). Today the headquarters of the Hillforest Historical Foundation, this house could have been suggested by the Regency style in early nineteenth-century England.*

ABOVE: *Saint James Church, Grosse Ile, Michigan, 1867 (Gordon W. Lloyd).*
BELOW: *Mitchell-Turner house, Milan, Ohio, 1847–48 (architect unknown).*

*Residence of John S. Moffat, Hudson, Wisconsin, c. 1865 (architect unknown). In 1968 the headquarters of the Saint Croix Valley Historical Society, the Moffat house is an excellent Midwestern example of the octagon style, popularized in the 1850s by Orson Squire Fowler and his brother Lorenzo. Fowler had been famous as a phrenologist before he turned his attention to the* home for all, *as he called his octagons.*

ABOVE: *Residence of Charles H. Lewis, Hudson, Wisconsin, c. 1865 (architect unknown).* BELOW: *Residence of J. Russell Jones, Galena, Illinois, 1857 (architect unknown). For those who shied away from Gothic cottages, there was always the Italian villa, of which style the Jones house may be the best example in Illinois.*

ABOVE: *Residence of John M. Wheeler, Ann Arbor, Michigan, c. 1851 (architect unknown).* BELOW: *Old State Bank, Shawneetown, Illinois, 1839 (architect unknown). The Gothic specimen from Ann Arbor has been now altered out of recognition, but the Grecian temple in southern Illinois has survived.*

*Doorway, the Avery-Downer house, Granville, Ohio, 1838–42*
*(Benjamin Morgan).*

# "THINGS VERY ANCIENT NEVER, FOR SOME MYSTERIOUS REASON, APPEAR VULGAR"

*Residence of Benjamin Franklin Allen, Des Moines, Iowa, 1869 (W. W. Boyington). There may be no more dramatic example in the United States of the mansardic style so popular in the 1860s and 1870s. Allen was a banker who went bankrupt.*

"Things very ancient never, for some mysterious reason, appear vulgar," wrote Henry James on contemplating the mansion of Jacques Coeur at Bourges. This comment could be made also about many an American monument in the hectic years following the Civil War.

Two views of the Chicago Water Tower, Michigan Avenue at Chicago Avenue, Chicago, Illinois, 1869 (W. W. Boyington). The Water Tower, which miraculously survived the Great Chicago Fire, is a building dear to all Chicagoans. It was guilty of amusing Oscar Wilde on his inspection of the city in 1883.

*Van Wert County Courthouse, Van Wert, Ohio, 1875–76 (Thomas J. Tolan). Aesthetes may shudder, but it is a fact that most great monuments are memorials to ambition. There may be no more ambitious courthouse in America than this mansardic example.*

ABOVE: *Residence of N. K. Fairbank, Lake Geneva, Wisconsin, 1874 (Treat & Foltz).* BELOW: *The Fairbank living room. Nathaniel Kellogg Fairbank, the creator of Santa Claus soap, was a familiar face at the Millionaires' Table of the Chicago Club. He chose the architects of the old Chicago Club (now demolished) for his summer home at Lake Geneva.*

ABOVE: *Gazebo, residence of Alexander Mitchell, Milwaukee, Wisconsin, c. 1870 (architect unknown). The Mitchell residence serves as the headquarters of the Wisconsin Club.*

BELOW: *Residence of Cyrus Hall McCormick, Chicago, Illinois, 1879 (Cudell & Blumenthal). In this mansardic palace, now destroyed, the inventor of the reaper staged in 1880 a magnificent coming-of-age party for his first-born, Cyrus Hall McCormick II. On that evening an orchestra led by Julius Fuchs gave Chicago its first performance of Goldmark's* Rustic Wedding.

ABOVE: *Eads Bridge, Saint Louis, Missouri, 1867–74 (James Buchanan Eads)*. BELOW: *Pillsbury "A" Mill, Minneapolis, Minnesota, 1880 (L. S. Buffington). Eads was an engineer who remains a legendary figure to all architects. Buffington was an architect who will never be forgotten by architectural historians: he claimed to have invented the skyscraper, but his patent was proved fraudulent by Professor Dimitri Tselos. The dates on the pertinent drawings were faked.*

ABOVE: *The Palmer House, Chicago, Illinois, 1873 (John Mills Van Osdel).* BELOW: *The Palmer House dining room. Now replaced by the hotel bearing the same name, this was the second Palmer House to be seen on State Street: it replaced the original, which disappeared in the Great Chicago Fire. The owner, Marshall Field's former partner Potter Palmer, found that Cyrus Hall McCormick was a difficult guest in the dining room. The inventor of the reaper insisted on a cut rate for dinner. Said Palmer to McCormick, fearing that the news might spread: "The price that we agreed upon for dinners I wish confined to yourself only, for the reason that 75 cents does not pay me the actual cost of dinners."*

21

The Chicago Architectural Photographing Co.

*Marshall Field Wholesale Store or Warehouse, Chicago, Illinois, 1885–87. Now demolished, this building, which stood on the block bounded by Wells, Franklin, Quincy and Adams Streets, haunted Louis Sullivan and many another Chicago architect. Richardson died with Field's name on his lips, whispering to the doctor that he longed "to live two years to see the Pittsburgh Court House and the Chicago store complete." On those two works he felt his reputation would stand.*

OPPOSITE ABOVE: *Residence of Marshall Field, 1905 Prairie Avenue, Chicago, Illinois, 1873 (Richard Morris Hunt).* BELOW: *Residence of William Borden, 1020 Lake Shore Drive, Chicago, Illinois, 1884 (Richard Morris Hunt). Both these mansions have been demolished. When Marshall Field gave a party in 1885 for his son Marshall Field II and his daughter Ethel (later the wife of Admiral Beatty), the favors were designed in London by none other than James McNeill Whistler. It was in the Borden castle that Adlai E. Stevenson courted his wife, William Borden's granddaughter.*

23

ABOVE: *Residence of Franklin MacVeagh, Chicago, Illinois, 1885–87.* BELOW: *Residence of John J. Glessner, 1800 Prairie Avenue, Chicago, Illinois, 1885–87. The MacVeagh house, now destroyed, was the fortress on Lake Shore Drive of the wholesale groceries dealer who became Taft's Secretary of the Treasury. The Glessner house, occupied in 1968 by the Chicago School of Architecture Foundation, was the monument of a pioneer in the farm machinery business; his concern, like that of McCormick, was ultimately merged in International Harvester.*

*Doorway, residence of John J. Glessner, 1800 Prairie Avenue, Chicago, Illinois, 1885–87.*

# WILSON EYRE, JR.

Residence of Charles Lang Freer, 71 East Ferry Avenue, Detroit, Michigan, c. 1887. The finest example in the Middle West of the so-called shingle style popularized by McKim, Mead & White at Newport, the Freer house serves in 1968 as headquarters of the Merrill-Palmer Institute for training teachers for young children. Freer, who made his money building railroad cars, was the friend and patron of James McNeill Whistler. Here, in an annex, was stored Whistler's Peacock Room before it was removed to the Freer Gallery in Washington.

ABOVE: *Presbyterian Church, Lake Forest, Illinois, 1886.* BELOW: *Former Chicago Historical Society Building, northwest corner of Dearborn and Ontario Streets, Chicago, Illinois, 1892.*

*A devoted Richardsonian when he designed the Chicago Historical Society and the Newberry Library nearby, Cobb eventually turned to a somewhat scholarly version of the Gothic for the early buildings of the University of Chicago.*

*Residence of Clement Studebaker, 600 West Washington Street, South Bend, Indiana, 1886. This wagon manufacturer was known to have entertained Presidents Grant, Harrison and McKinley.*

*Cobb's partner in the design of this Richardsonian landmark and of the Palmer residence was Charles S. Frost.*

*Residence of Potter Palmer, Lake Shore Drive at Banks Street, Chicago, Illinois, 1882. "The age of Pericles seems to be dawning in Chicago," the* Inter-Ocean *saluted this angry Gothic castle. Boni de Castellane, who called on Mrs. Palmer before his marriage to Jay Gould's daughter, was not so easily pleased. On penetrating the porte-cochère, he pronounced the castle "sumptuous and abominable." It is now demolished.*

*Residence of James J. Hill, 240 Summit Avenue, Saint Paul, Minnesota, 1891. Although Hill chose an Eastern firm to design his mansion (in 1968 occupied by the Archdiocese), he never lost sight of the importance of Chicago. In Chicago he never failed to call on Marshall Field. "He has the damndest eyes," the master of the Great Northern Railroad told Field's nephew. "I go in there to ask him a question, and by the time I've come out, I've told him all I know. He pumps me dry."*

*Doorway, Mabel Tainter Memorial, Menomonie, Wisconsin, 1889. This community center was built in honor of the daughter of the local lumber magnate Andrew Tainter. Harvey Ellis was a marvelous draftsman and an incorrigible alcoholic. This meant that his talent was spent not on his own fame but on that of the firms for which he worked, and not until a careful examination has been made of the production of J. Walter Stevens in Saint Paul, L. S. Buffington in Minneapolis, and Eckel & Mann in Saint Louis and Saint Joseph, Missouri, may his exact contribution be defined. Just such an examination is being made by Roger G. Kennedy. It seems certain, however, in 1968 that Ellis was the author not only of the Tainter Memorial but also of the Motter and McAllister houses in Saint Joseph and Washington Terrace in Saint Louis.*

ABOVE: *Mabel Tainter Memorial, Menomonie, Wisconsin, 1889.* BELOW: *Doorway, residence of Joshua Motter, Saint Joseph, Missouri, 1890.*

32

ABOVE: *Residence of James W. McAllister, Saint Joseph, Missouri, 1890.* BELOW: *Detail, gates to Washington Terrace, Saint Louis, Missouri, 1893.*

*Hotel Florence, Pullman, Illinois, 1881. Named for Pullman's daughter, later the wife of Governor Lowden.*

*The failings of the model town were exposed during the Pullman strike of 1894. "The damned idiot ought to arbitrate, arbitrate and arbitrate!" roared that eminent and sensible Republican Mark Hanna. A friend spoke of all the fine things Pullman had done for his workmen in the model town. "Oh, hell!" said Hanna. "Model ———! Go and live in Pullman and find out how much Pullman gets sellin' city water and gas to those poor fools! . . . A man who won't meet his own men halfway is a God-damn fool!" When Pullman died in the fall of 1897, leaving an estate of $17,400,000, his family, perhaps because they feared reprisals from wayward employees, buried him with care, embedding his coffin in asphalt and binding it down by steel rails through which no ghoul could hope to claw. In 1968 the Pullman plant has been abandoned by the Pullman Co.*

OPPOSITE ABOVE: *Pullman Works, Pullman, Illinois, 1881.* BELOW: *Pullman housing, Pullman, Illinois, 1881.*

*Assisted by I. K. Pond, Beman was responsible for the model town on the South Side constructed by the inventor of the lower and upper berths.*

35

*Home Insurance Building, southwest corner of LaSalle and Adams Streets, Chicago, Illinois, 1883. This candidate for the distinction of being the world's first skyscraper was erected during the decade in which Loop property soared from $130,000 the quarter-acre to $900,000. The Home Insurance has been demolished.*

36

*Leiter Building I, northwest corner of Wells and Monroe Streets, Chicago, Illinois, 1879. As Carl Condit has pointed out, the First Leiter is very nearly a glass box. Although its brick piers are not essential bearing members, the outer floor beams are carried over to iron columns immediately inside the piers, which means the latter are freed from interior loads, making possible something resembling a glass envelope. Leiter I was originally five stories high; two more were added in 1888.*

# HOLABIRD & ROCHE

The Chicago Architectural Photographing Co.

*Tacoma Building, northeast corner of La Salle and Madison Streets, Chicago, Illinois, 1886–89. This second candidate for the distinction of being the first skyscraper was the first whose structural frame was riveted. Now demolished.*

LEFT: *The Monroe Building, southwest corner of Monroe Street and Michigan Avenue, Chicago, Illinois, 1912.* RIGHT: *The University Club, northwest corner of Monroe Street and Michigan Avenue, Chicago, Illinois, 1909. Although damned as "eclectic" by architectural historians who bristle at the slightest evidence of historicism, these skyscrapers remain an elegant addition to the Chicago skyline.*

*The Chicago Architectural Photographing Co.*

*The Monadnock Building, 53 West Jackson Boulevard, Chicago, Illinois, 1891–93. Root's first sketches were rejected as too ornate; in his absence Burnham suggested an uncompromising, unornamented façade. With this scheme Root in the end grandly agreed.*

*Woman's Temple, southwest corner of La Salle and Monroe Streets, Chicago, Illinois, 1891–92. This skyscraper, commissioned by the Women's Christian Temperance Union, has been demolished.*

ABOVE: *Masonic Temple (originally The Capitol Building), northwest corner of State and Randolph Streets, Chicago, Illinois, 1891–92. Now demolished, this twenty-two-story structure was the highest building in the world at the time.* BELOW: *Entrance to Rookery Building, 209 South La Salle Street, Chicago, Illinois, 1886–88. The lobby was remodeled by Frank Lloyd Wright in 1905 (see page 67).*

*The Chicago Architectural Photographing Co.*

*Frame of the stage of the Auditorium (as restored by Harry M. Weese).*

*Schiller Building, later the Garrick Theatre Building, 64 West Randolph Street,
Chicago, Illinois, 1891–92. In the foreground is the Borden Block, the work of
Dankmar Adler & Co., 1879–80. Both buildings have been demolished.*

Richard Nickel

*Interior of the theater in the Schiller Building.*

49

ABOVE: *Tomb of Martin Ryerson, Graceland Cemetery, Chicago, Illinois, 1889.*
BELOW: *Tomb of Charlotte Dickson Wainwright, Bellefontaine Cemetery, Saint Louis, Missouri, 1892.* Martin Ryerson—no relation of the E. L. Ryerson whose mansion in Lake Forest may be seen on page 110—was the father of the Martin A. Ryerson who gave so many Renoirs to the Art Institute of Chicago. Charlotte Dickson Wainwright was the wife of the brewer for whom Sullivan built the Wainwright Building (opposite).

Richard Nickel

*Wainwright Building, northwest corner of Seventh and Chestnut Streets, Saint Louis, Missouri, 1890–91.*

*Tomb of Carrie Eliza Getty, Graceland Cemetery, Chicago, Illinois, 1890.*

ABOVE: *Entrance to Stock Exchange Building, 30 North La Salle Street, Chicago, Illinois, 1894.* BELOW: *People's Savings & Loan Association Building, southeast corner of Court Street and Ohio Avenue, Sidney, Ohio, 1917–18.*

*Richard Nickel*

*Schlesinger & Mayer Department Store, southeast corner of State and Madison Streets, Chicago, Illinois, 1899–1904. Now occupied by Carson, Pirie Scott & Co. Original cornice removed.*

*Detail, entrance, Schlesinger & Mayer store. George Elmslie was responsible for the ornament in this instance.*

ABOVE: *Merchants National Bank (later Poweshiek County National Bank), northwest corner, Fourth Avenue and Broad Street, Grinnell, Iowa, 1914.* BELOW: *Farmers & Merchants Union Bank, northwest corner, James Street and Broadway, Columbus, Wisconsin, 1919.*

*National Farmers Bank, northeast corner, Broadway and Cedar Streets, Owatonna, Minnesota, 1908. George Elmslie was partly responsible for this design.*

ABOVE: *Detail, façade of the National Farmers Bank.* BELOW: *Interior. On the right may be seen part of the restoration and enlargement by Harwell Hamilton Harris in 1958.*

ABOVE: *Residence of Henry Babson, Riverside, Illinois, 1907.* BELOW: *Residence of Josephine Crane Bradley, 106 North Prospect Street, Madison, Wisconsin, 1909. The Babson house has been destroyed. The Bradley house in 1968 is the Sigma Phi Fraternity House.*

*William P. Krause Music Store and residence, 4611 North Lincoln Avenue, Chicago, Illinois, 1922. In 1968 the Arntzen-Coleman Funeral Home.*

60

The Chicago Historical Society

Administration Building (Richard Morris Hunt).

ABOVE: *Agricultural Building (McKim, Mead & White).* BELOW: *Manufactures Building (George B. Post).*

ABOVE: *Fisheries Building (Henry Ives Cobb).* BELOW: *Art Building (Charles B. Atwood). Resurfaced and recarved in limestone, the Art Building survives in 1968 as the Museum of Science and Industry in Jackson Park.*

*Transportation Building (Louis H. Sullivan). The Golden Doorway was not wholly original, as Professor Dimitri Tselos has recently proved. A possible precedent may be found in the Auguenaou Gate in Marrakech, Morocco.*

OPPOSITE ABOVE: *Residence of George Blossom, Chicago, Illinois, 1892.* BELOW: *Residence of Isidor Heller, Chicago, Illinois, 1897.*

*Residence of W. H. Winslow, River Forest, Illinois, 1893.*

OPPOSITE ABOVE: *Lobby of the Rookery, 209 South La Salle Street, Chicago, Illinois, 1905. (A view of the entrance is on page 42.)* BELOW: *Residence of James Charnley, Chicago, Illinois, 1891. Although attributed to Adler & Sullivan, there is every reason to believe that this is the work of Wright. Originally the house was symmetrical; the extreme right is an addition.*

67

*Residence of Ward W. Willitts, Highland Park, Illinois, 1902.*

OPPOSITE ABOVE: *Side view, Unitarian Universalist Church (Unity Temple), Lake Street at Kenilworth Avenue, Oak Park, Illinois, 1906.* BELOW: *Interior.*

*Front view, Unitarian Universalist Church (Unity Temple), Lake Street at Kenilworth Avenue, Oak Park, Illinois, 1906.*

OPPOSITE ABOVE: *Residence of F. F. Tomek, Riverside, Illinois, 1907.* BELOW: *Residence of Frank J. Baker, Wilmette, Illinois, 1909.*

*Residence of Frederick C. Robie, Chicago, Illinois, 1909.*

ABOVE: *Residence of P. A. Beachy, Oak Park, Illinois, 1906.* BELOW: *Residence of W. G. Fricke, Oak Park, Illinois, 1902.*

*Residence of Thomas P. Hardy, Racine, Wisconsin, 1905.*

OPPOSITE ABOVE: *Residence of W. E. Martin, Oak Park, Illinois, 1903.* BELOW: *Residence of Emil Balch, Chicago, Illinois, 1915.*

*Residence of B. Harley Bradley, Kankakee, Illinois, 1900.*

ABOVE: *Residence of Francis W. Little, Peoria, Illinois, 1903.* BELOW: *Residence of Warren Hickox, Kankakee, Illinois, 1900.*

*Residence of Avery Coonley, Riverside, Illinois, 1908. The Coonley house has
now been altered beyond recognition.*

OPPOSITE ABOVE: *Living room, residence of Avery Coonley.* BELOW: *Playhouse for
residence of Avery Coonley, Riverside, Illinois, 1912. The Coonley playhouse
has also been altered.*

The Chicago Architectural Photographing Co.

ABOVE: *Residence of E. H. Cheney, Oak Park, Illinois, 1904.* BELOW: *Residence of Susan L. Dana, Springfield, Illinois, 1903.*

*Midway Gardens, Cottage Grove Avenue at 60th Street, Chicago, Illinois, 1914.*
*Demolished.*

ABOVE: *Residence of Mayer May, Grand Rapids, Michigan, 1909.* BELOW: *Residence of E. A. Gilmore, Madison, Wisconsin, 1908.*

82

*Studio, Taliesin East, residence of Frank Lloyd Wright, Spring Green, Wisconsin,
1925–1959.*

ABOVE: *Far view, Taliesin East, residence of Frank Lloyd Wright, Spring Green, Wisconsin, 1925–1959.* BELOW: *Entrance.*

ABOVE: *Entrance, Carl Schurz High School, northeast corner of Milwaukee and Addison Avenues, Chicago, Illinois, 1909 (Dwight H. Perkins).* BELOW: *Side view. A graduate of the office of Burnham & Root, Perkins became the chief architect of the Chicago Board of Education.*

85

*The Chicago Architectural Photographing Co.*

*Chapin & Gore Building, 63 East Adams Street, Chicago, Illinois, 1904 (Hugh M. G. Garden in the office of Richard E. Schmidt). The Canadian Hugh M. G. Garden was to join the Bavarian-born Richard E. Schmidt and the structural engineer Edgar Martin to form the firm of Schmidt, Garden & Martin in 1906. The Chapin & Gore Building has been altered since this photograph was taken.*

ABOVE: *Montgomery Ward Warehouse, 618 West Chicago Avenue, Chicago, Illinois, 1907 (Schmidt, Garden & Martin). This is the largest building of the Chicago School to be supported on a reinforced concrete frame.* BELOW: *Residence of Albert F. Madlener, Chicago, Illinois, 1902 (Richard E. Schmidt).*

*Residence of Robert Herrick, Chicago, Illinois, 1900 (Hugh M. G. Garden).*
*Herrick, who taught at the University of Chicago, was the author of one of the*
*superior Chicago novels,* Memoirs of an American Citizen.

ABOVE: *Residence of Robert Mueller, Decatur, Illinois, 1910 (Marion Mahony and Hermann von Holst).* BELOW: *Residence of J. H. Amberg, Grand Rapids, Michigan, 1910 (Marion Mahony and Hermann von Holst). Marion Mahony, perhaps the most gifted draftsman on Wright's staff, was to become the wife of Walter Burley Griffin. To her and Von Holst, Wright entrusted these and other commissions in the office when he and Mamah Borthwick Cheney (the Cheney house is shown on page 80) set off for Europe, abandoning the Wright and Cheney households in Oak Park.*

*Residence of J. G. Melson, Mason City, Iowa, 1913 (Walter Burley Griffin).*
*Griffin, another of Wright's assistants, won the international competition for the*
*planning of Canberra, the capital of Australia, and spent the rest of his life there*
*and in India.*

OPPOSITE ABOVE: *Residence for Hurd Comstock, Evanston, Illinois, 1912 (Walter*
*Burley Griffin).* BELOW: *Residence of Harry Page, Mason City, Iowa, 1913*
*(Walter Burley Griffin).*

*Stinson Library, Anna, Illinois, 1914 (Walter Burley Griffin).*

*Residence of J. F. Clarke, Fairfield, Iowa, 1915 (Barry Byrne). Yet another graduate of the Wright office, Byrne was later to make his reputation as the architect of many Roman Catholic churches.*

*Residence of George W. Maher, Kenilworth, Illinois, 1893 (George W. Maher).*

OPPOSITE ABOVE: *Joseph Sears School, Kenilworth, Illinois, 1912 (George W. Maher).* BELOW: *Kenilworth Club, Kenilworth, Illinois, 1907 (George W. Maher). Maher, who worked in the office of J. L. Silsbee at Wright's side before the latter joined Adler & Sullivan, was most respected for the boulder-hewn residence of the grain speculator James A. Patten in Evanston, Illinois, and for the Patten Gymnasium given to Northwestern University. Both of these buildings in Evanston have been destroyed.*

95

*Winona Savings Bank, Winona, Minnesota, 1916 (George W. Maher). Here Maher seems to have been tempted by the classic revival advocated by Burnham.*

*Residence of J. Hall Taylor, Oak Park, Illinois, 1913 (George W. Maher).*

*Brookfield Kindergarten, Brookfield, Illinois, c. 1912 (Guenzel & Drummond).*
*Louis Guenzel was a German who got his start in the office of Adler & Sullivan.*
*His partner, William Drummond, was once one of Wright's assistants. Together*
*they designed this kindergarten (since converted to a private residence) for one*
*of Mrs. Avery Coonley's experiments in children's education.*

OPPOSITE ABOVE: *First Congregational Church of Austin (in 1968 Our Lady of*
*Lebanon Church), 5701 West Midway Park Avenue, Chicago, Illinois, 1908*
*(William Drummond).* BELOW: *Thorncroft, Riverside, Illinois, 1912 (Guenzel*
*& Drummond). This building was erected to house teachers Mrs. Coonley*
*engaged.*

*Women's Club, 526 Ashland Avenue, River Forest, Illinois, 1913 (Guenzel & Drummond).*

*Woodbury County Courthouse, corner of Seventh and Douglas Streets, Sioux City, Iowa, 1915–17 (Purcell & Elmslie in association with William L. Steele). The firm of Purcell & Elmslie (or Purcell, Feick & Elmslie as it was known from 1909 to 1913 when George Feick was also a partner) was steeped as was no other in the tradition of Louis Sullivan. William Gray Purcell had served in Sullivan's office before joining that of John Galen Howard in Berkeley, California. George Grant Elmslie, with Adler & Sullivan at the time Wright came to work there, remained at Sullivan's right hand until 1909, assisting him with the decoration of the Schlesinger & Mayer store, and helping plan the National Farmers Bank at Owatonna.*

*Entrance, First National Bank, 8 West Davenport Street, Rhinelander, Wisconsin, 1910–11 (Purcell, Feick & Elmslie).*

*Residence of William Gray Purcell, Minneapolis, Minnesota, 1913 (Purcell & Elmslie).*

*Merchants National Bank of Winona, corner of Third and Lafayette Streets, Winona, Minnesota, 1911–12 (Purcell, Feick & Elmslie).*

*Residence of Harold C. Bradley, Madison, Wisconsin, 1914–15 (Purcell & Elmslie).*

*Garage and service buildings for residence of Henry Babson, Riverside, Illinois, 1915–16 (Purcell & Elmslie).*

*Residence of Alden B. Dow, Midland, Michigan, 1935–41.*
*A graduate of the University of Michigan and of the Columbia University School*
*of Architecture, Dow also studied under Frank Lloyd Wright at Taliesin.*

ABOVE: *Ragdale, residence of Howard Van Doren Shaw, Lake Forest, Illinois, 1897 (Howard Van Doren Shaw).* BELOW: *Market Square, Lake Forest, Illinois, 1913 (Howard Van Doren Shaw). The most distinguished Chicago eclectic— that is, the most distinguished Chicago architect who referred to historical precedent in his work—was Howard Van Doren Shaw, many of whose finest achievements may be seen in Lake Forest. The Market Square, an unusually graceful shopping center, was commissioned by a group of businessmen headed by Cyrus Hall McCormick II.*

ABOVE: *Residence of T. E. Donnelley, Lake Forest, Illinois, 1911 (Howard Van Doren Shaw).* BELOW: *Residence of Prentiss Coonley, Lake Forest, Illinois, 1908 (Howard Van Doren Shaw). T. E. Donnelley was president of the printing firm of R. R. Donnelley & Sons. Prentiss Coonley was the brother of Wright's client in Riverside.*

ABOVE: *Entrance, residence of E. L. Ryerson, Lake Forest, Illinois, 1913 (Howard Van Doren Shaw)*. BELOW: *Side view. In 1968 the steel magnate's mansion serves the needs of Saint Bonaventure's Novitiate, Order of Friars Minor.*

*Residence of Stanley Keith, Lake Forest, Illinois, 1931 (David Adler). No relation of Dankmar Adler, David Adler was trained in the office of Shaw. As Christopher Tunnard has reminded us, the architects of Lake Forest owe a debt to David Hotchkiss, who laid out the romantic plan of the town in 1856, a decade before Frederick Law Olmsted did similar work at Riverside.*

*Tribune Tower, North Michigan Avenue at Chicago River, Chicago, Illinois, 1922–25 (John Mead Howells and Raymond Hood). Eliel Saarinen placed second in the gloriously advertised competition for the Tribune Tower.*

*Detroit Institute of Arts, 5200 Woodward Avenue, Detroit, Michigan, 1927* (Paul-Philippe Cret et al.).

ABOVE: *Capitol, Saint Paul, Minnesota, 1896–98 (Cass Gilbert).* BELOW: *Detroit Public Library, 5201 Woodward Avenue, Detroit, Michigan, 1917–21 (Cass Gilbert).*

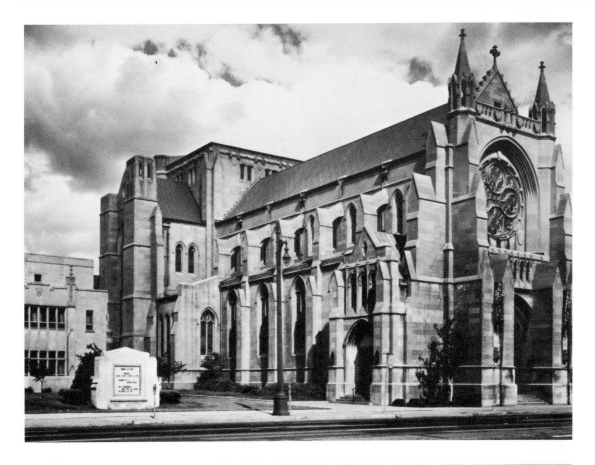

ABOVE: *Saint Paul's Cathedral, 4800 Woodward Avenue, Detroit, Michigan, 1911–19 (Ralph Adams Cram).* BELOW: *Christ Church Cranbrook, Bloomfield Hills, Michigan, 1924 (Bertram G. Goodhue Associates). Saint Paul's lacks the tower for which Cram pleaded. Christ Church Cranbrook was to have been designed by Goodhue; on his death it was completed by his office.*

*Howard Hall, Principia College, Elsah, Illinois, 1935 (Bernard R. Maybeck).*

*Anderson Hall, Principia College, Elsah, Illinois, 1935 (Bernard R. Maybeck). Whether Maybeck was a complete eclectic may be doubted. The inventiveness of his Christian Science Church in Berkeley, California, has enchanted many a modern architect in the 1960s.*

116

ABOVE: *Villa Turicum, residence of Mr. and Mrs. Harold Fowler McCormick, Lake Forest, Illinois, 1908 (Charles A. Platt).* BELOW: *Garden Temple for Villa Turicum. Frank Lloyd Wright had hoped to win this commission, but his plans were rejected in favor of those of Platt, whose work was a charming ruin by the time these photographs were taken. Villa Turicum has since been demolished.*

117

*Residence of Russell A. Alger, Jr., Grosse Pointe, Michigan, 1910 (Charles A. Platt). Built for the son of McKinley's Secretary of War, this mansion serves in 1968 as the Grosse Pointe War Memorial.*

OPPOSITE ABOVE: *Entrance, Gwinn, residence of William Gwinn Mather, Cleveland, Ohio, 1907 (Charles A. Platt).* BELOW: *Gate lodge for Gwinn. William Gwinn Mather was president of the Cleveland-Cliffs Iron Co. Platt was the most talented of all the Eastern eclectics who worked in the Middle West. Gwinn may be the most distinguished house in Cleveland.*

ABOVE: *S. C. Johnson Administration Building, Racine, Wisconsin, 1936–39.*
BELOW: *Interior of the Administration Building. Virtually ignored in the conservative 1920s, Wright staged a comeback in 1936 when he built not only this temple for Johnson Wax but also Falling Water near Pittsburgh for E. J. Kaufmann.*

*Research Tower for S. C. Johnson Co., Racine, Wisconsin, 1951.*

*Miss Johnson's wing, Wingspread, residence of Herbert F. Johnson, Jr., Racine, Wisconsin, 1937. In 1968 Wingspread serves as the headquarters of the Wingspread Foundation.*

OPPOSITE: *Interior and exterior, First Unitarian Meeting House, Madison, Wisconsin, 1951.*

*Apse, First Unitarian Meeting House, Madison, Wisconsin, 1951.*

*Residence of Curtis Meyer, Galesburg Village, Michigan, 1951.*

*Residence of William Palmer, Ann Arbor, Michigan, 1951.*

*Residence of Herbert Jacobs, Jr., Middleton, Wisconsin, 1950.*

*Annunciation Greek Orthodox Church, Wauwatosa, Wisconsin, 1955–61.*

*Residence of Carl Schultz, Saint Joseph, Michigan, 1958.*

ABOVE: *Residence of Lowell Walter, Quasqueton, Iowa, 1949.* BELOW: *Boathouse for residence of Lowell Walter.*

ABOVE: *Residence of Ina Morriss Harper, Saint Joseph, Michigan, 1951.* BELOW: *Residence of Kenneth Laurent, Rockford, Illinois, 1951.*

*Residence of Douglas Grant, Cedar Rapids, Iowa, 1951.*

OPPOSITE: *Interior and exterior, residence of Harry Neils, Minneapolis, Minnesota, 1952.*

*Detail of exterior, residence of Harry Neils, Minneapolis, Minnesota, 1952.*

*Front and rear, residence of H. T. Mossberg, South Bend, Indiana, 1952.*

*Interior, residence of H. T. Mossberg, South Bend, Indiana, 1952.*

OPPOSITE ABOVE: *Residence of Mrs. W. C. Alpaugh, Northport, Michigan, 1948–49.* BELOW: *Residence of Melvyn Maxwell Smith, Bloomfield Hills, Michigan, 1951. The addition to the left in the Alpaugh house is the work of Glen T. Arat & Associates.*

ABOVE: *Residence of Carroll Alsop, Oskaloosa, Iowa, 1951.* BELOW: *Residence of Charles F. Glore, Lake Forest, Illinois, 1955.*

*Exterior and interior, residence of Dr. A. T. Miller, Charles City, Iowa, 1952.*

137

*Residence of Dr. Richard M. Davis, Marion, Indiana, 1954.*

OPPOSITE: *Exterior and interior, residence of Bernard Schwarz, Two Rivers, Wisconsin, 1939.*

*Residence of Richard Smith, Jefferson, Wisconsin, 1951.*

*General Motors Building, West Grand Boulevard at Cass, Detroit, Michigan, 1920.*

"*When I began,*" *Kahn claimed,* "*the real architects would design only museums, cathedrals, capitols, monuments. The office boy was considered good enough for factories. I'm still that office boy designing factories. I have no dignity to be impaired.*" *But Kahn was more than a factory designer. Detroit's greatest monument may be the General Motors Building, in which he followed the classical precedent of D. H. Burnham.*

*William L. Clements Library, Ann Arbor, Michigan, 1923. This was Kahn's favorite of all his buildings.*

*General Library, University of Michigan, Ann Arbor, Michigan, 1918.*

*Dodge Half-Ton Truck Plant, Warren, Michigan, 1938. Since this photograph was taken, considerable alterations have been made.*

OPPOSITE ABOVE: *Residence of Edsel B. Ford, Grosse Pointe, Michigan, 1929.* BELOW: *Entrance drive, residence of Edsel B. Ford. The landscaping of the Ford estate was the work of Jens Jensen.*

144

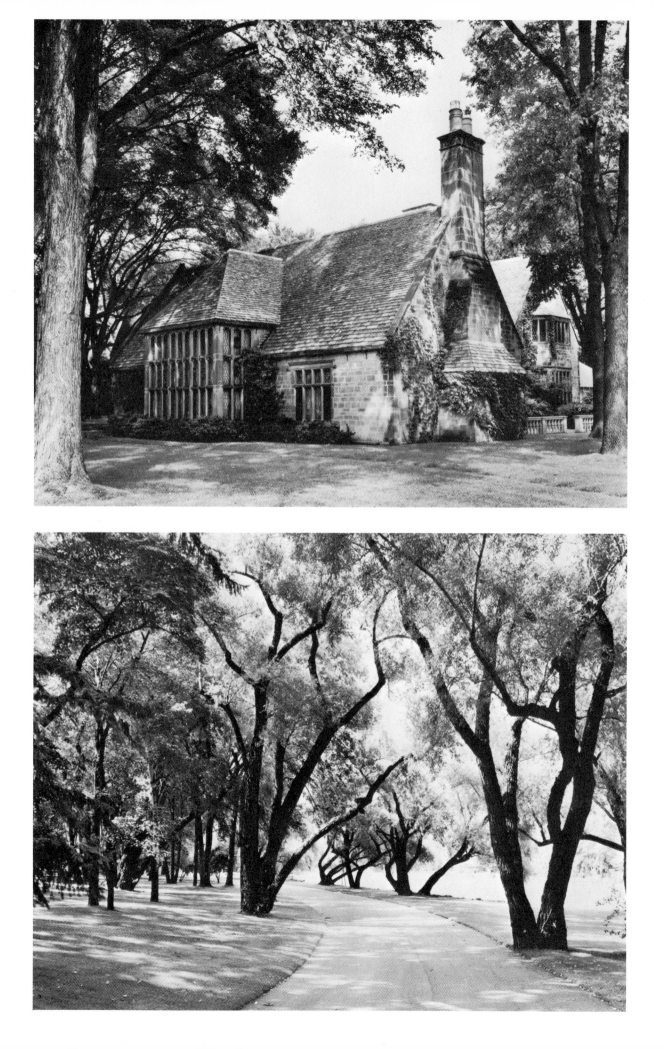

*Kingswood School for Girls, Bloomfield Hills, Michigan, 1929.*

OPPOSITE ABOVE: *Colonnade, Cranbrook Academy, Bloomfield Hills, Michigan, 1940.* BELOW: *Orpheus Fountain, Cranbrook Academy, 1936 (Carl Milles).*

147

*Detail, courtyard, Kingswood School for Girls, Bloomfield Hills, Michigan, 1929.*

OPPOSITE ABOVE: *Dining room, Kingswood School for Girls, Bloomfield Hills, Michigan, 1929.* BELOW: *Front hall, Kingswood School.*

149

*Crow Island School, Winnetka, Illinois, 1939–40. Here the Saarinens collaborated with Perkins, Wheeler & Will.*

OPPOSITE ABOVE: *Tabernacle Church of Christ, Columbus, Indiana, 1940–42.* BELOW: *Interior.*

*Two views of Concordia College, Fort Wayne, Indiana, 1954–58.*

*Jefferson Westward Expansion Memorial, Saint Louis, Missouri, 1948. In the background may be seen the Eads Bridge.*

153

*Staircase, Styling Building, General Motors Technical Center, Warren, Michigan, 1948–56.*

OPPOSITE ABOVE: *Styling Building, General Motors Technical Center, Warren, Michigan 1948–56.* BELOW: *Engineering Building, General Motors Technical Center, Warren, Michigan, 1948–56. On this commission Saarinen was associated with Smith, Hinchman & Grylls.*

*International Business Machines Office Buildings, Rochester, Minnesota, 1956.*

OPPOSITE: *Two views, John Deere & Co., Headquarters, Moline, Illinois, 1964.*

*Close-up, John Deere & Co. Headquarters, Moline, Illinois, 1964.*

*Crown Hall, Illinois Institute of Technology, Chicago, Illinois, 1956.*

*Carman Hall, Illinois Institute of Technology, Chicago, Illinois, 1954.*

160

ABOVE: *Saint Savior's Chapel, Illinois Institute of Technology, Chicago, Illinois, 1952.* BELOW: *Memorial Hall, Illinois Institute of Technology, Chicago, Illinois, 1946.*

161

ABOVE: *Home Federal Building, Des Moines, Iowa, 1962.* BELOW: *School of Social Service Administration Building, 969 East 60th Street, Chicago, Illinois, 1964.*

*Lake View–Fullerton Apartments, Chicago, Illinois, 1963.*

163

*Commonwealth Promenade Apartments, Diversey Avenue and Sheridan Road, Chicago, Illinois, 1957.*

*High-rise apartments, Lafayette Park, Detroit, Michigan, 1961.*

*Town houses, Lafayette Park, Detroit, Michigan, 1961.*

*860–880 Lake Shore Drive, Chicago, Illinois, 1952.*

167

*Federal Center, Dearborn from Adams to Jackson, Chicago, Illinois, 1964–67. Here Miës was the associate of Schmidt, Garden & Erikson, C. F. Murphy Associates, and A. Epstein and Sons.*

*Residence of Dr. Edith Farnsworth, Plano, Illinois, 1950.*

ABOVE: *Inland Steel Building, 30 West Monroe Street, Chicago, Illinois, 1957.* BELOW: *Administration Building, University of Illinois at Chicago Circle, Chicago, Illinois, 1967. Walter A. Netsch was the partner in charge of this project.*

*Hedrich Blessing*

170

*Close-up (with Picasso) of Civic Center, block bounded by Randolph, Washington, Dearborn and Clark, Chicago, Illinois, 1964–65. The complete credit line reads: C. F. Murphy Associates, Loebl, Schlossman & Bennett, and Skidmore, Owings & Merrill.*

171

ABOVE: *McGregor Community Conference Center, Wayne State University, Detroit, Michigan, 1958.* BELOW: *Conservatory of Music, Oberlin College, Oberlin, Ohio, 1964.*

ABOVE: *Saint John's Abbey Church, Collegeville, Minnesota, 1962.* BELOW: *Church of Saint Francis de Sales, Muskegon, Michigan, 1967. Herbert Beckhard was Breuer's associate on the latter commission.*

173

# BERTRAND GOLDBERG

ABOVE: *Marina Apartments, north bank of Chicago River, between State and Dearborn Streets, Chicago, Illinois, 1964 (Bertrand Goldberg Associates).*
BELOW: *Tyrone Guthrie Theater, Minneapolis, Minnesota, 1963 (Ralph Rapson).*

# RALPH RAPSON

174

ABOVE: *Housing for Hyde Park redevelopment, Chicago, Illinois, 1958.* BELOW: *Stanley R. Pierce Hall, University of Chicago, Chicago, Illinois, 1959–60. Weese was associated with I. M. Pei and Loewenberg & Loewenberg in the Hyde Park redevelopment.*

*Leco Photo Service and R. Buckminster Fuller*

*Climatron, Botanical Gardens, Saint Louis, Missouri, 1960.*

*Leco Photo Service and R. Buckminster Fuller*

*Leco Photo Service and R. Buckminster Fuller*

*Interior and exterior, residence of R. Buckminster Fuller, Carbondale, Illinois, 1960. Since 1959 this most ingenious engineer has been teaching at Southern Illinois University.*

*Residence of John B. Swainson and Patrick Whitehead, Manistee, Michigan, 1966.*

OPPOSITE ABOVE: *Student Center, Olivet College, Olivet, Michigan, 1962.* BELOW: *Entrance, Lake Michigan Hall, Grand Valley State College, Allenville, Michigan, 1967.*

# BIBLIOGRAPHY

The complete file of *The Prairie School Review*, 1964–  , is an absolute necessity. This astonishing magazine, dedicated to the delightful proposition that everyone should be interested in the work of Frank Lloyd Wright and his contemporaries, is edited by W. R. Hasbrouck, 117 Fir Street, Park Forest, Illinois.

Andrews, Wayne, *Architecture, Ambition and Americans*, New York, 1955.
——, *Architecture in America*, New York, 1960.
——, *Architecture in Michigan*, Detroit, 1967.
——, *Battle for Chicago*, New York, 1946.
Barford, George, and Stanley G. Wold, eds., *Architecture in Illinois*, Springfield, 1964.
Birrell, James, *Walter Burley Griffin*, St. Lucia (Queensland, Australia), 1964.
Bragdon, Claude, "Harvey Ellis," *Architectural Review*, December, 1908.
Burnham Library of Architecture, *Buildings by Frank Lloyd Wright in Seven Middle Western States*, Chicago, 1963.
Christison, Muriel B., "How Buffington Staked His Claim," *Art Bulletin*, March, 1944.
Christ-Janer, Albert, *Eliel Saarinen*, Chicago, 1948.
Cleveland Chapter, American Institute of Architects, *A Guide to Cleveland Architecture*, New York, 1958.
Condit, Carl W., *The Chicago School of Architecture*, Chicago, 1964.
——, *The Rise of the Skyscraper*, Chicago, 1952.
Connelly, Willard, *Louis Sullivan as He Lived*, New York, 1960.
Cooper, Mabel Ruth, *Nineteenth Century Homes of Marshall, Michigan*, unpublished doctoral dissertation, Tallahassee, 1963.
Drexler, Arthur, *Ludwig Miës van der Rohe*, New York, 1962.
Eaton, Leonard K., *Landscape Artist in America: The Life and Work of Jens Jensen*, Chicago, 1965.
Egbert, Donald D., "In Search of John Edelman, Architect and Anarchist," *Journal of the American Institute of Architects*, February, 1966.
Farr, Finis, *Frank Lloyd Wright*, New York, 1961.
Ferry, W. Hawkins, "The Gothic and Tuscan Revivals in Detroit: 1828–1875," *Art Quarterly*, Summer, 1946.
——, "The Mansions of Grosse Pointe," *Monthly Bulletin of the Michigan Society of Architects*, March, 1956.
——, "Representative Detroit Buildings: A Cross Section of Architecture 1832–1943," *Bulletin of the Detroit Institute of Arts*, March, 1943.
Flanders, Robert B., *Nauvoo: Kingdom on the Mississippi*, Chicago, 1965.
Frary, I. T., *Early Homes of Ohio*, Richmond, 1936.
Fuller, R. Buckminster, *Ideas and Integrities: A Spontaneous Autobiographical Disclosure*, Englewood Cliffs, 1963.
Gebhard, David, ed., *The Work of Purcell & Elmslie*, Prairie School Press, 1965 (a reprint of *Western Architect* for January, 1913, January, 1915, and July, 1915).
Hitchcock, Henry-Russell, *The Architecture of H. H. Richardson and His Times*, New York, 1936.
——, *In the Nature of Materials 1887–1941: The Buildings of Frank Lloyd Wright*, New York, 1943.
Hoffmann, Donald, ed., *The Meanings of Architecture: Buildings and Writings by John Wellborn Root*, New York, 1967.
Jacobus, John M., *Philip Johnson*, New York, 1962.
Johannesen, Eric, "Simeon Porter: Ohio Architect," *Ohio History*, Summer, 1956.
Johnson, Philip C., *Miës van der Rohe*, New York, 1947.
Jordy, William H., and Ralph Coe, eds., *American Architecture and Other Writings by Montgomery Schuyler*, 2 vols., Cambridge, 1961.
Kaufmann, Edgar, Jr., *Louis Sullivan and the Architecture of Free Enterprise*, Chicago, 1956.
Kaufmann, Edgar, Jr., and Ben Raeburn, eds., *Frank Lloyd Wright: Writings and Buildings*, Cleveland, 1960.
Kennedy, Roger G., "Houses of the St. Croix Valley," *Minnesota History*, December, 1963.
——, "The Long Shadow of Harvey Ellis," *Minnesota History*, Fall, 1966.
——, *Minnesota Houses*, St. Paul, 1967.

Koeper, H. F., *Historic Saint Paul Buildings*, St. Paul, 1964.

"Making a Monument Work," *Architectural Forum*, July, 1958 (on the restoration of the Sullivan bank at Owatonna).

Manson, Grant C., *Frank Lloyd Wright to 1910*, New York, 1958.

McHale, John, *R. Buckminster Fuller*, New York, 1962.

McKee, Harley J., "Glimpses of Architecture— Michigan," *Michigan History*, March, 1966.

Monroe, Harriet, *John Wellborn Root*, Boston, 1896 (reissued 1966 by the Prairie School Press, Park Forest, Ill.).

Moore, Charles H., *Daniel H. Burnham*, 2 vols., Boston, 1921.

Morrison, Hugh S., "Buffington and the Invention of the Skyscraper," *Art Bulletin*, March, 1944.

——, *Louis Sullivan*, New York, 1935.

Nelson, George, *The Industrial Architecture of Albert Kahn*, New York, 1939.

Newcomb, Rexford G., *Architecture of the Old Northwest Territory*, Chicago, 1950.

Oak Park Public Library, *A Guide to the Architecture of Frank Lloyd Wright in Oak Park and River Forest, Illinois*, Oak Park, 1966.

Ohio Historical Society, *Ohio Historic Landmarks*, Columbus, 1967.

——, *Zoar: An Experiment in Communalism*, Columbus, 1966.

Peat, Wilbur D., *Indiana Houses of the Nineteenth Century*, Indianapolis, 1962.

Peisch, Mark L., *The Chicago School of Architecture: Early Followers of Sullivan and Wright*, New York, 1964.

Pickens, Buford L., "Treasure Hunting at Detroit," *Architectural Review*, December, 1944.

Rudd, J. William, *et al.*, eds., *Historic American Buildings Survey: Chicago and Nearby Areas*, Chicago, 1956.

Saarinen, Aline B., ed., *Eero Saarinen on His Work*, New Haven, 1962.

Scully, Vincent, Jr., *Frank Lloyd Wright*, New York, 1960.

Siegel, Arthur, ed., *Chicago's Famous Buildings*, Chicago, 1965.

Smith, Norris Kelly, *Frank Lloyd Wright: A Study in Architectural Content*, New York, 1966.

Sullivan, Louis H., *The Autobiography of an Idea*, New York, 1924.

——, *Democracy*, Detroit, 1961.

——, *Kindergarten Chats*, New York, 1947.

——, *A System of Architectural Ornament*, New York, 1924.

Swales, Francis S., "Harvey Ellis," *Pencil Points*, July, 1924.

Tallmadge, Thomas E., *Architecture in Old Chicago*, Chicago, 1941.

Temko, Allan, *Eero Saarinen*, New York, 1962.

Torbert, Donald R., *A Century of Art and Architecture in Minnesota*, Minneapolis, 1958.

——, *A Century of Minnesota Architecture*, Minneapolis, 1958.

Tselos, Dimitri, "The Enigma of Buffington's Skyscraper," *Art Bulletin*, March, 1944.

——, "Exotic Influences in the Work of Frank Lloyd Wright," *Magazine of Art*, April, 1953.

Tunnard, Christopher, *The City of Man*, New York, 1953.

"Tyrone Guthrie Theater," *Design Quarterly 58*, Minneapolis, 1963.

Upjohn, Everard M., "Buffington and the Skyscraper," *Art Bulletin*, March, 1944.

Webster, J. Carson, *Architecture of Chicago and Vicinity*, Society of Architectural Historians, Media, Pa., 1965.

Wright, Frank Lloyd, *An Autobiography*, New York, 1932.

——, *Drawings for a Living Architecture*, New York, 1959.

——, *Frank Lloyd Wright on Architecture*, edited by Frederick Gutheim, New York, 1941.

——, *The Future of Architecture*, New York, 1953.

——, *Genius and the Mobocracy*, New York, 1949.

——, *The Living City*, New York, 1958.

——, *The Natural House*, New York, 1954.

——, *A New House on Bear Run, Pennsylvania, by Frank Lloyd Wright*, New York, 1938.

——, *The Story of the Tower*, New York, 1956.

——, *Taliesin Drawings*, New York, 1952.

——, *A Testament*, New York, 1931.

Wright, John Lloyd, *My Father Who Is on Earth*, New York, 1946.

# INDEX (ARCHITECTS IN ITALICS)

73 74 75   12 11 10 9 8 7 6 5 4 3 2 1

# WAYNE ANDREWS

Born in Kenilworth, Illinois, in 1913, Mr. Andrews was educated in the Winnetka public schools, Lawrenceville School, and Harvard College. Later he received his doctorate in American history at Columbia University under the sponsorship of Allan Nevins. From 1948 to 1956 he was Curator of Manuscripts at the New York Historical Society. From 1956 to 1963 he was an editor at Charles Scribner's Sons. Since 1964 he has been Archives of American Art Professor at Wayne State University, Detroit.

Mr. Andrews is the author of *The Vanderbilt Legend* (1941), *Battle for Chicago* (1946), *Architecture, Ambition and Americans* (1955), *Architecture in America* (1960), *Germaine: A Portrait of Madame de Staël* (1963), *Architecture in Michigan* (1967), *Architecture in Chicago and Mid-America* (1968), *Architecture in New York* (1969), *Siegfried's Curse: The German Journey from Nietzsche to Hesse* (1972) and *Architecture in New England* (1973). He is also the editor of *The Best Short Stories of Edith Wharton* (1958), and under the pseudonym Montagu O'Reilly is the author of *Who Has Been Tampering with These Pianos?* He has contributed to such publications as *The Architectural Review, Town and Country, House Beautiful, House and Garden, Harper's, Harper's Bazaar, The Saturday Review* and *The New York Times*. He is also a former president of the New York chapter of the Society of Architectural Historians.

## Icon Editions

W9-BJB-007

# my Book 1

## Authors and Advisors

Alma Flor Ada • Kylene Beers • F. Isabel Campoy

Joyce Armstrong Carroll • Nathan Clemens

Anne Cunningham • Martha C. Hougen

Elena Izquierdo • Carol Jago • Erik Palmer

Robert E. Probst • Shane Templeton • Julie Washington

## Contributing Consultants

David Dockterman • Mindset Works®

Jill Eggleton

**HMH** | **into Reading™**

Texas

*my* **Book** 1

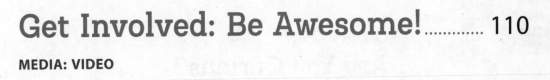

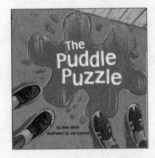

# Be a Super Citizen

"You've got to give more than you take."

—Christopher Reeve

# How can being a good citizen make a difference to others?

Get Curious Video

# Words About Citizenship

Complete the Vocabulary Network to show what you know about the words.

## citizen

**Meaning:** A **citizen** is a member of a community, state, or country.

**Synonyms and Antonyms**

Drawing

## difference

**Meaning:** When people make a **difference**, they do something that helps others.

| Synonyms and Antonyms | Drawing |
|---|---|
| | |

## kind

**Meaning:** Someone who is **kind** is nice, caring, or gentle.

| Synonyms and Antonyms | Drawing |
|---|---|
| | |

# We Are ★ SUPER CITIZENS ★

My dog Bailey is the best! When we learned about good citizens in school, my teacher asked us to think of ways we could be good citizens. I thought about Bailey. She's friendly and gentle. I just knew she could be a good therapy dog.

First, I found a dog club near where I live. My mom and I took Bailey there. Bailey took a test to see how she behaved. She was calm and acted well with strangers. She listened to commands.

After some training classes, we became a therapy dog team. Now my mom and I take Bailey to visit people. Bailey gives them comfort and love.

I like raising a therapy dog. We are good citizens together. Bailey makes a difference in the lives of the people we visit. She helps make their lives better.

## FAST FACT

Therapy dogs are not the same as service dogs. Service dogs are trained to provide a certain kind of help for a person with special needs.

# Prepare to Read

**GENRE STUDY** **Fantasies** are stories with made-up events that could not really happen. As you read *Clark the Shark,* look for:

- animal characters who talk and act like people
- the beginning, middle, and end of the story
- how pictures and words help you understand what happens

**SET A PURPOSE** **Ask questions** before, during, and after you read to help you get information or understand the text. Look for evidence in the text and pictures to answer your questions.

**POWER WORDS**

munch

bellowed

rough

handle

cool

bounce

grinned

might

Meet Bruce Hale.

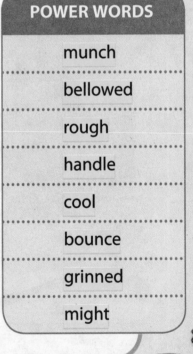

# CLARK THE SHARK

by Bruce Hale

illustrated by
Guy Francis

In all the wide blue seas, in all the wide blue world,
the top school for fish was Theodore Roosterfish Elementary.
And of all the fish at Theodore Roosterfish, the biggest and
the strongest was Clark the Shark.

Clark loved school, and he loved his teacher, Mrs. Inkydink. He loved to play upsy-downsy and spinna-ma-jig with his friends. Clark *loved* his life.

**"SCHOOL IS AWESOME!"** shouted Clark the Shark.

"Less shouting, more reading," said Mrs. Inkydink.

18

**"LUNCHTIME IS SWEEEEET!"**

yelled Clark the Shark.

"Munch your *own* lunch," said his best friend, Joey Mackerel.

**"RECESS ROCKS!"** bellowed Clark the Shark.

"You are playing rough, Clark!"

19

Yes, Clark loved his life with all of his sharky heart. But he loved everything *way* too much.

He was too loud.

He was too wild.

He was just too much shark for the other fish to handle.

After a while, no one would play with Clark. No one ate lunch with him. No one sat with him at circle time. Even his best friend, Joey Mackerel, said, "Cool your jets, Clark! You're making me crazy!"

5-2=

20

One day, Clark asked Mrs. Inkydink, "What's *wrong* with everyone?"

Mrs. Inkydink patted his fin. "Clark, sometimes you play too hard, you munch too hard, and—gosh—you even help too hard."

"But life is SO exciting!" said Clark.

"There's a time and a place for everything," said Mrs. Inkydink. "And sometimes the rule is *stay cool*."

STAY COOL!

At recess, Clark tried to stay cool, but he pushed the swing with too much zing! "Sorry," said Clark. "I forgot."

"Yikes!" cried Joey Mackerel.

At lunch, Clark tried to stay cool, but everything smelled so good that he munched a bunch of lunches.

"Sorry," said Clark. "I forgot."

"We're STARVING!" said his friends.

In class, Clark tried to stay cool, but a good book got him all shook up.

"Now, Clark!" said Mrs. Inkydink. "This isn't the time or the place. Tell me, what's the rule?"

"Stay cool," said Clark.

"Hey, that rhymes!" he cried.

Then Clark got a big idea in his sharky head. *Maybe if I make a rhyme, I'll remember every time!* he thought. The next day, he put his plan to work.

In class, when lessons got exciting, Clark wanted to bounce up out of his seat.

Instead, he told himself: "When teacher's talking, don't go walking."

And what do you know? It worked!

"Attaboy, Clark!" said Mrs. Inkydink.

Clark smiled. "Lessons are fun!"

NaCl + H₂O =

SCIE

At lunch, everything smelled *sooo* yummy. When Clark wanted to eat
and eat and never stop, he told himself: "Only munch your own lunch."
And it worked again!
"Way to go, Clark!" said his friends.
Clark grinned. "Lunch is fun."

At playtime, Clark told himself: "Easy does
it, that's the way.

"Then my friends will let me play."

And playtime was fun. Once more, Clark
loved his life.

But then a shadow fell across the playground—a *gi-normous* shadow with tentacles galore. "It's a new kid, and he looks scary!" cried Joey Mackerel. "Swim for your lives!"

The squid squashed the slide, and it snapped off the swings.

"Oops. My bad," said the new kid.

"Wait," said Clark. "He just wants to play. Let's find a way!"

And he swam at the new kid with all his might. Clark played harder than he ever had before—upsy-downsy and spinna-ma-jig.

Why, he even made up a new game: tail-whump-a-lumpus!

"Wow, that was fun," said the new kid breathlessly, and he settled down.
"If you want to come to school, you've got to stay cool," said Clark.

"That's right, Clark," said Mrs. Inkydink. "And thanks for taking care of our new classmate, Sid the Squid."

"Hooray for Clark the Shark!" everyone cheered.

That night Clark's mother asked, "What did you learn at school, dear?"

"There's a time and a place for everything," Clark said. "Sometimes you stay cool."

"But sometimes a shark's gotta do what a shark's gotta do."

## Turn and Talk

Use details from *Clark the Shark* to answer these questions with a partner.

1. **Ask and Answer Questions** What questions did you ask yourself about Clark before, during, and after reading? How did your questions help you understand the story?

2. Why do Clark's friends stop playing with him? How do you think that makes him feel? Use details in the text and pictures to explain your ideas.

3. Choose one of Clark's rhyming rules. Explain how it helps him to be a good citizen.

## Talking Tip

Your ideas are important! Be sure to speak loudly and clearly as you share them.

# Write a Description

**PROMPT**  How do you know that Clark wants to do the right thing? Use details from the words and pictures to explain your ideas.

**PLAN**  First, think about the story. Then draw a scene that shows Clark trying to do the right thing.

**WRITE** Now, write sentences to describe a time when Clark tries to do the right thing. Remember to:

- Find details in the story that explain your idea.

- Use describing words to tell what Clark does or tries to do.

_____

_____

_____

_____

_____

_____

_____

_____

_____

_____

# Prepare to Read

GENRE STUDY **Fantasies** are stories with made-up events that could not really happen.

MAKE A PREDICTION Preview "A Forest Welcome." Sunny Bunny is moving into a new home. What do you think will happen when she meets her neighbors?

_____

_____

_____

_____

_____

_____

SET A PURPOSE Read to find out what happens when Sunny Bunny moves to her new home.

# A Forest Welcome

**READ** What is the setting of the story? <u>Underline</u> it.

All morning, Sunny Bunny hopped cheerily around the forest. Finally, she stopped near a pretty tree and grinned. She had found the perfect spot to make her new home. *Scritch, scratch.* Sunny's little bunny claws quickly dug at the dirt. A raccoon was resting high up in the tree and heard Sunny Bunny.

"Welcome to the neighborhood," he said. "I am Roy Raccoon, and I am a great digger. Let me help you!" ▶

> **Close Reading Tip**
> Put a **?** by the parts you have questions about.

---

**CHECK MY UNDERSTANDING**

Why is the setting of the story important?

_____

_____

**37**

**Close Reading Tip**

Put a ! by a surprising part.

**READ** Which animals help Sunny? <u>Underline</u> their names.

"I am Sunny Bunny," Sunny said to her new friend. "It's nice to meet you, Roy!"

When Barb Bear heard there was a new bunny in town, she threw a big party to welcome Sunny. All the forest animals came. Sunny was thrilled to make so many new friends. When the party ended, it was quite late. Sunny was not sure she could find her way home. Sid Skunk said not to worry because he could see in the dark. He led Sunny all the way home. When she was snug in bed, Sunny smiled. She was going to like her new home!

**CHECK MY UNDERSTANDING**

What questions did you ask yourself before, during, and after reading? How did your questions help you understand the story?

_____

_____

_____

_____

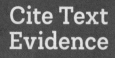

**WRITE ABOUT IT** Write a short thank-you note from Sunny to one of her new friends. Describe what the character did and how it made Sunny feel. Use details from the story in your answer.

_____

_____

_____

_____

_____

_____

_____

_____

_____

_____

_____

# Prepare to Read

**GENRE STUDY** **Fantasies** are stories with made-up events that could not really happen. As you read *Spoon,* look for:

- characters who are not found in real life
- the setting, or where the story takes place
- a lesson the main character learns

**SET A PURPOSE** As you read, stop and think if you don't understand something. Reread, ask yourself questions, use what you already know, and look for visual clues to help you understand the text.

**POWER WORDS**

proper

blue

useful

realize

**Meet Amy Krouse Rosenthal.**

# SPOON

by Amy Krouse Rosenthal          illustrated by Scott Magoon

This is Spoon.

This is Spoon's family.

On Sundays, Spoon goes to visit his Aunt Silver.
He has to be on his very best behavior there.
She's very fancy and proper.

"Good-bye, darling!
Ta, ta!"

44

At bedtime, Spoon likes to hear the story about his adventurous great-grandmother, who fell in love with a dish and ran off to a distant land.

Lately, though, Spoon had been feeling blue.
"What's wrong?" asked his mother. "You look a
bit out of shape."

"Nothing," mumbled Spoon.

"It's just that . . . I don't know . . .
All my friends have it so much better than me.

Like Knife.
Knife is so lucky!
He gets to cut,
he gets to spread.
I never get to cut or spread."

"Yes, Knife is pretty spiffy that way, isn't he?"

"And Fork, Fork is so lucky! She gets to go practically EVERYWHERE. I bet she never goes stir-crazy like I do."

"Fork does get out and make herself useful, doesn't she?"

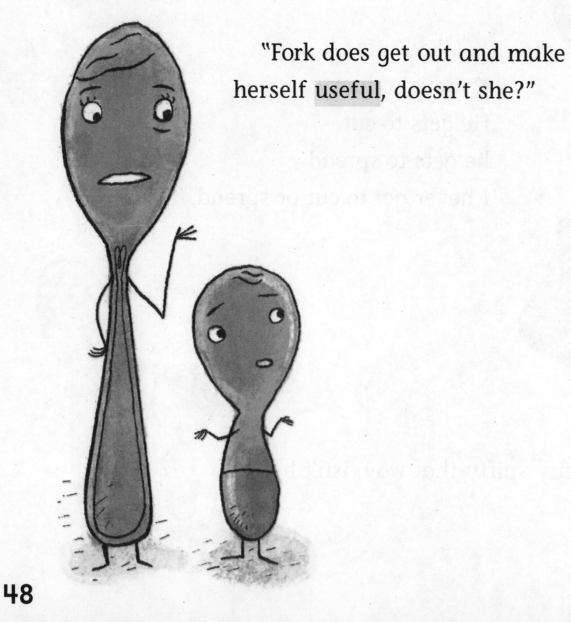

"And Chopsticks! They are so lucky!
Everyone thinks they're really cool and exotic.
No one thinks I'm cool or exotic."

"Those Chopsticks are
something else, aren't they?"

Meanwhile . . . if only Spoon knew what his friends were saying at that very minute!

"Spoon is so lucky!" said Knife. "He's so fun and easygoing. Everyone's so serious with me; no one's ever allowed to be silly with me like they are with Spoon."

"Spoon is so lucky!" said Fork. "He gets to measure stuff. No one ever does that with me."

"Spoon is so lucky!" said Chopsticks. "He can go places by himself. We could never function apart."

That night after bedtime stories, Spoon's mom turned off the light, tucked him in, and said . . .

"You know, Spoon—I wonder if you realize just how lucky you are.

"Your friends will never know
the joy of diving headfirst into
a bowl of ice cream."

"They'll never know what it feels like to clink against the side of a cereal bowl.

"They'll never be able to twirl around in a mug, or relax in a hot cup of tea."

Spoon hadn't thought of it that way before. He lay awake in bed for a long time. His mind was racing . . . he felt so alive!

There was only one thing to do.

"I can't sleep."

"Come, snuggle."

"Come, Spoon."

And so he did.

58

Use details from *Spoon* to answer these questions with a partner.

1. **Monitor and Clarify** What did you do when you came to a part of the text that you didn't understand? Tell how it helped or didn't help you.

2. Which details in the words and pictures help you understand why Spoon feels better at the end of the story?

3. What does this story teach you about being yourself?

## Listening Tip

Look at your partner as you listen. Wait until your partner finishes speaking before you talk.

# Write an Opinion

**PROMPT** In your opinion, which character in *Spoon* has the most important job? Look for details in the words and pictures to help you decide.

**PLAN** First, write which character you chose in the chart. Then write or draw reasons why you chose that character.

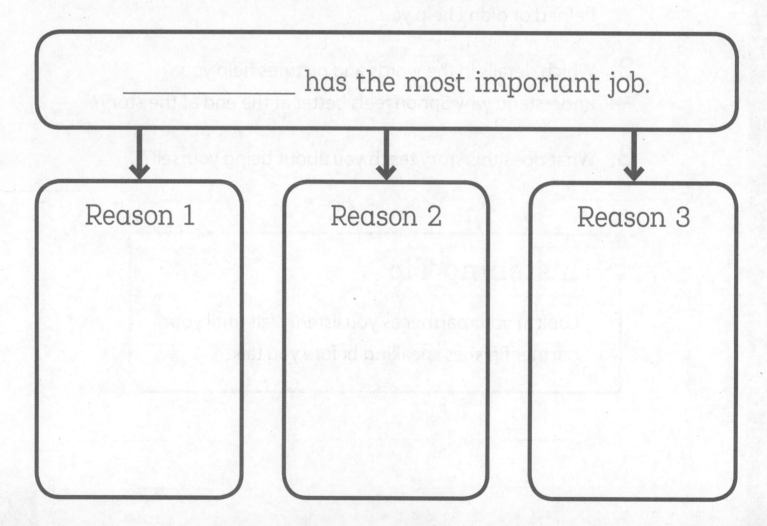

_____ has the most important job.

| Reason 1 | Reason 2 | Reason 3 |

**WRITE**  Now write your opinion about the character you chose.
Include reasons that tell why you think that character has the
most important job. Remember to:

- Use opinion words like *I believe* or *I think*.

- Use words like *and, because,* and *also* to tell more about
  your reasons.

**SPOON**

by Amy Krouse Rosenthal        Illustrated by Scott Magoon

_____

_____

_____

_____

_____

_____

_____

_____

_____

# Prepare to Read

**GENRE STUDY** **Fantasies** are stories with made-up events that could not really happen.

**MAKE A PREDICTION** Preview "Fly Like an Eagle." There is trouble in this nest. You have learned that the setting is an important part of a story. What do you think the setting in this story will be like?

_____

_____

_____

_____

_____

_____

**SET A PURPOSE** Read to find out what the setting is like and to see if your prediction is right. If not, use what you know about story settings to make a new prediction.

# Fly Like an Eagle

**READ** What do you think *squabbling* means? Use the text and picture for help.

---

It was a bright, sunny day. High up in a tree, in a big nest, a

brother and sister eaglet were squabbling.

"What is the problem here?" asked Mama Eagle.

"He called me a symbol," said Sister Eagle.

"You *are* a symbol," said her brother.

"My little eaglets, you are both symbols," Papa Eagle said. ▶

**Close Reading Tip**

Mark important words with *.

### CHECK MY UNDERSTANDING

Which details from the story tell you it is made up?

_____

_____

63

**READ** As you read, ask yourself questions about parts that don't make sense. Then go back and reread those parts.

**Close Reading Tip**

Put a ? by the parts you have questions about.

"Being a symbol is something you can be proud of," Mama Eagle explained. "It means you stand for something."

The two eaglets were confused. They weren't standing. They were sitting!

"Eagles are symbols for this great country of ours," said Papa Eagle. "We are free to fly anywhere we wish. We remind people that they are also free. We are big and strong. We remind people that our country is also big and strong. Being a symbol means we stand for, or represent, something else."

"That's so cool!" said Brother Eagle.

"Wow," Sister Eagle said. "I am proud to be a symbol."

**CHECK MY UNDERSTANDING**

What is the author's purpose for writing this story?

_____

_____

_____

**WRITE ABOUT IT**   "Fly Like an Eagle" is a fantasy about eagles and why they are important to us. How does the author make it fun to read? Use details from the story in your answer.

_____

_____

_____

_____

_____

_____

_____

_____

_____

_____

_____

# Prepare to Read

**GENRE STUDY** **Informational text** is one kind of nonfiction. It gives facts about a topic. As you read *Being a Good Citizen*, look for:

- main topic and details
- photographs
- facts about events

**SET A PURPOSE** As you read, **summarize** the text. Use your own words to describe the most important ideas in an order that makes sense.

## POWER WORDS

elected

local

mock

compliment

Build Background: Ways to Help Your Community

# Being a Good Citizen

by Rachelle Kreisman

with illustrations by Tim Haggerty

# Community Living

Everyone is part of a community. A community is a place where people live, work, and play. Each community is made up of neighborhoods. Those neighborhoods are made up of people. You are one of those people! So you are part of a community.

Good citizens make the community a better place. A citizen is a person who lives in a certain place. It can be a town or city, state, or country.

How can you be a good citizen? Make a difference in your community! Learn about your elected officials and follow rules. Get involved in community activities. Be a good neighbor and help others. Do you want to learn more? Of course, you do! Keep reading to find out more about how you can be a good citizen.

## JUST JOKING!

**Q:** How did the ocean greet its neighbor?

**A:** It waved!

# Get Involved

**G**ood citizens are involved in the community. They get to know their neighbors and other citizens. They work to make their community a better place to live.

What can you do to get involved? Start by taking part in after-school activities. Join a community center or youth group. They have programs and activities just for kids. You can have fun and make new friends.

**JUST JOKING!**

**Q:** Did you hear the joke about the community center's roof?

**A:** Never mind—it's over your head!

After-school activities can be a good way to try new things.

Another way to get involved is to follow local news. That will let you know what is going on in your community. For example, you might learn that your police department is teaching a free bike safety class. Maybe you will want to take the class.

How can you follow the news? Read school and local newspapers. Watch the local news with a parent. Then talk about what you learned. Ask family members their opinions and share your own.

Being a good citizen includes voting. Citizens can vote in local, state, and national elections. You must be 18 years old to vote in most states.

Every four years, citizens elect the president of the United States. Kids can vote too! How? Many schools invite kids to take part in a mock election. It helps students learn about the election process.

**DID YOU KNOW?**
People in the United States vote on Election Day. It is always the Tuesday after the first Monday in November.

How else can you get involved? Learn about your community history. Visit museums and town landmarks. Go with a parent to take a tour of your city hall. Meet some of your elected officials. Attend a school board meeting.

Some schools have a student council. They organize special activities and help make school decisions. If you have a student council, you can vote to elect officers. You may also want to serve on the council!

Most museums welcome students.

73

# Help Others

Good citizens are active in community service. They volunteer their time to help others. They also donate items and money to people in need. That can make a big difference in people's lives.

Helping others can make a difference in your life too. It can bring you a lot of joy! Doing good deeds can inspire others to do the same.

**FUN FACT**
Doing a kind act can make you just as happy as receiving one. Both affect your brain in the same way. They make your brain give off feel-good chemicals, say scientists.

What can you do to help others? Start by doing random acts of kindness. Those acts are small, kind gestures. For example, draw a picture for a friend or family member. Say a friendly "hello" to a neighbor. Give flowers to a teacher. Hold the door open for the next person. Read a book to a younger child. Give someone a compliment.

You can do random acts of kindness every day. See how many kind acts you can do for others.

Being a good citizen helps make your community a better place. It also makes you feel good about yourself. Are you ready?

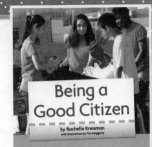

Use details from *Being a Good Citizen* to answer these questions with a partner.

1. **Summarize** What have you learned about good citizens from reading this text?

2. Find three questions the author asks readers. Why do you think she asks questions instead of just telling the facts?

3. Use details from the text to tell how helping in the community can also help you.

## Talking Tip

Use details from the text to explain your ideas. Complete the sentence below.

I read that _____.

# Write Directions

**PROMPT**  If someone asked you for directions about how to be a good citizen, what would you tell him or her? Use details from the words and pictures to explain your ideas.

**PLAN**  First, think of three steps to follow to be a good citizen. Write or draw them below.

| Step 1 | Step 2 | Step 3 |
|---|---|---|
|  |  |  |

**WRITE** Now write directions that tell how to be a good citizen.
Be sure your directions are easy to follow. Remember to:

- Choose the most important details in the text.

- Use action words that tell your readers exactly what to do.

_____

_____

_____

_____

_____

_____

_____

_____

_____

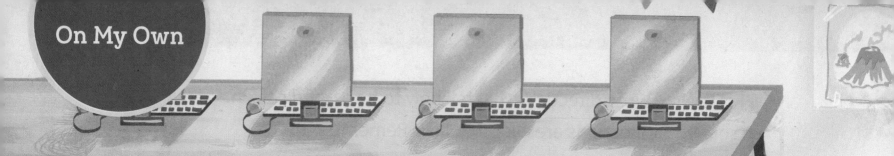

# Prepare to Read

**GENRE STUDY** **Informational text** is nonfiction. It gives facts about a topic.

**MAKE A PREDICTION** Preview "Be a Good Digital Citizen." You know that informational text has facts. What do you think you will learn from this text?

_____

_____

_____

_____

_____

_____

**SET A PURPOSE** Read to find out what the author wants you to know about being a good digital citizen.

# Be a Good Digital Citizen

**READ** What are digital citizens? <u>Underline</u> the sentence that tells you.

Every time people go online, they become part of the online community. They might be on social media or sending emails. They might just be surfing the web.

Digital citizens are people who work or play in the online community. Just like in other communities, there are rules that should be followed. ▶

**Close Reading Tip**

Mark important words with a *.

### CHECK MY UNDERSTANDING

What is the author's main purpose for writing this page of text?

_____

_____

_____

81

**READ** As you read, think about what rules digital citizens follow. <u>Underline</u> three rules.

Children can be digital citizens, too. Some rules help keep children safe. Children should always ask a trusted adult before going online. They should only go to websites that are approved. Children should tell an adult if they see something online that bothers them.

All digital citizens should talk online the way they would talk in person. They should use kind words and be respectful. They should not use words that may hurt someone's feelings.

These rules keep the online community a safe place to work and play!

**CHECK MY UNDERSTANDING**

Which important ideas from the text would you use in a summary?

_____

_____

_____

**WRITE ABOUT IT** What other things can you do to be a good digital citizen? Write two more ideas. Use details from the text in your answer.

_____

_____

_____

_____

_____

_____

_____

_____

_____

_____

_____

# Prepare to Read

**GENRE STUDY** **Realistic fiction** stories are made up but could happen in real life. As you read *Picture Day Perfection,* look for:

- the beginning, middle, and end of the story
- characters who act and talk like real people
- problems that real people might have
- ways pictures and words help readers understand the story

**SET A PURPOSE** As you read, **create mental images,** or make pictures in your mind, to help you understand details in the text.

**POWER WORDS**

planned

perfect

hamper

disaster

scowl

mood

queasy

fiddled

**Meet Deborah Diesen.**

# PICTURE DAY PERFECTION

by Deborah Diesen      illustrated by Dan Santat

I'd planned for months. This was going to be the
year of the perfect school picture.
 But some days, not everything goes according
to plan.

The day started with the worst case of bedhead *ever*.

EXHIBIT A: FRONT VIEW

EXHIBIT C: BACK VIEW

EXHIBIT B: SIDE VIEW

EXHIBIT D: THE LOOK ON MY BROTHER'S FACE WHEN HE SAW MY HAIR.

Then it took me *quite* some time to unearth my favorite shirt. I finally found it at the *very* bottom of the hamper.

You might call it "stained."
You might call it "wrinkled."
You might even call it "smelly."
You wouldn't be wrong.

Breakfast was "Picture Day Pancakes," a family tradition.
This year's festivities involved a small syrup disaster.

89

More accurately described as a *large* syrup disaster.

And it occurred exactly as the bus pulled up.

I had a feeling we'd be getting a new family tradition.

On the bus, I got into a small bit of trouble.

Make that a *large* bit of trouble. The bus driver made me sit in the seat *right behind him* for the rest of the ride.

By the time I got into school, my picture day face was fixed in a scowl.

In class, Mrs. Smith collected our photo order forms. Do you think my mom checked "Emerald Green" for my photo background? Or "Peacock Blue?" Or "Pizzazzy Purple"?

No. Once again, of all the backgrounds in the world, Mom checked snoring-boring "Traditional Gray."

*No one* gets "Traditional Gray."

BACKGROUND COLOR
CHOOSE ONE:

Except for me.

And it just so happens to be the only color in
the world that makes my favorite shirt disappear.
All but the stains and the wrinkles.

93

After that, the teacher had us all stand up and practice our Picture Day smiles. Personally, I thought we needed a little something to get us in the Picture Day mood.

Whoops!
Got myself in trouble.

*Again.*

Luckily, I got to rejoin the class in time for Art.
Art involved quite a lot of paint.
Or at least it did for *me*.

95

Finally, it was time to line up for our photos.

Ned, just in front of me, got the *last* complimentary plastic comb.

I watched as classmate after classmate smiled for the camera. I got queasy listening to everyone say "Cheese."

I can't *stand* cheese.

The mere thought of it turns me green! *Deeply* green. And just as my face reached its most *awful* pea-green shade, it was . . . *my turn*.

I stepped forward.

I sat down on the stool.

It was hard as a rock, and cold as an iceberg.

"Just a sec," said the photographer
as he fiddled with the camera knobs.

As I sat and waited, everything that had happened rushed through my mind. The monstrous messes. The muddles and the mix-ups. The whole day, from the moment I'd rolled out of bed, had gone . . .

**PERFECTLY!**

*Even better than planned! This year, I was finally going to have the perfect school picture.*

99

And that's when I heard a

# CLICK!

In a flash, all my hard work—

my perfectly tangled hair,
my perfectly rumpled shirt,
my perfectly sticky face,
my perfectly composed scowl,
that perfect boring background,
those perfect paint splatters,
that perfect sickly pallor—

# WASTED!
# USELESS!
# *RUINED*,

in a moment of weakness,
by an unexpected smile.
Mom says it's my best picture ever.

But just *wait* till she sees *next* year's.

## Turn and Talk

Use details from *Picture Day Perfection* to answer these questions with a partner.

1. **Create Mental Images** What does the boy want his school photo to look like? Use details in the text to help you picture it in your mind. Then describe your picture to a partner.

2. What was the author's purpose for writing this story? Why do you think she called it *Picture Day Perfection?*

3. How is the boy different from characters you've read about recently? Explain whether you think he learns a lesson.

### Talking Tip

Complete the sentence to ask your partner for more information about an answer.

Tell me more about _____.

# Write a Sequel

**PROMPT**  Use what you know about the boy in *Picture Day Perfection* to write sentences about what he might do on next year's picture day. Look for details in the words and pictures to help you think of ideas.

**PLAN**  First, draw a picture of one thing the boy might try next year. Add a caption to describe what the boy is doing.

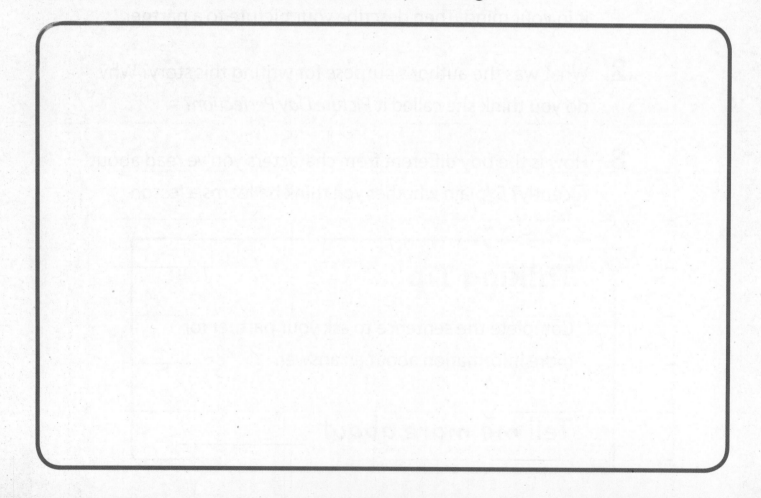

**WRITE** Now write your sequel! Explain what you think the boy's plan will be for next year's picture day. Remember to:

- Look for details in the story that give clues about what the boy might do next year.

- Write details that describe what the boy is thinking, feeling, and hoping.

_____

_____

_____

_____

_____

_____

_____

_____

_____

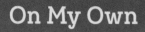

# Prepare to Read

GENRE STUDY **Realistic fiction** stories are made up but could happen in real life.

MAKE A PREDICTION Preview "Picture This!" In this story, a girl comes up with a plan to raise money. What do you think her plan will be?

_____

_____

_____

_____

_____

_____

_____

SET A PURPOSE Read to find out more about the girl and her plan to raise money.

# Picture This!

**READ** Which words help you picture what the yard looks like that Saturday? <u>Underline</u> them.

The local animal shelter needed money. I had a great idea! I could have a car-and-dog wash. Mom and Dad said they would help. It was going to be a lot of work.

"You'll be *sor*-ry!" my older sister sang out.

On Saturday, we were in the front yard surrounded by buckets and hoses. Our sign read *Save the Animal Shelter!* ▶

**Close Reading Tip**

Mark important ideas with a *.

**CHECK MY UNDERSTANDING**

What does the girl's older sister think about the plan?

_____

_____

**Close Reading Tip**

Circle the important describing words.

**READ** How does the girl feel about her day? <u>Underline</u> the words that are clues.

---

People started to arrive. The bookstore owner showed up. Then the mail carrier and baker got here. Everyone in town seemed to have a car or dog that needed washing. We were so busy!

Even my sister decided to lend a hand. Some of my friends showed up to help, too! We were all wet and soapy. The dogs and the cars were all sparkling clean, though!

"We should get a picture," someone said. "The shelter would love a picture with all the clean dogs!"

*Yes!* The day turned out just as I'd hoped!

**CHECK MY UNDERSTANDING**

Which details help you create a mental picture of the car-and-dog wash?

_____

_____

_____

**WRITE ABOUT IT** "Picture This!" is a story about a girl who wants to help her community. What kind of person do you think she is? Write a few sentences about her for the town newspaper. Use details from the story in your answer.

_____

_____

_____

_____

_____

_____

_____

_____

_____

_____

_____

_____

# Prepare to View

**GENRE STUDY** **Videos** are short movies that give you information or something for you to watch for enjoyment. As you watch *Get Involved: Be Awesome!*, notice:

- how pictures, sounds, and words work together
- what the video is about
- how the video makes you feel
- what the video is trying to persuade you to do

**SET A PURPOSE** Think about the video's **central idea.** Can you figure out its message? Think about how that message helps you understand what it means to be a good citizen.

**Build Background: Making a Difference**

Get Involved:
BE AWESOME!

**As You View** Are you ready to make your mark? Listen for details about how to become involved in your community. How do the ideas in the video help you understand what it means to be a super citizen?

## Turn and Talk

Use details from *Get Involved: Be Awesome!* to answer these questions with a partner.

1. **Central Idea**  What message does the video share? What does the girl try to persuade you to do?

2. What does the girl mean when she says "make your mark"?

3. The girl says to keep trying when things get tough. Do you think that is good advice? Explain why or why not.

## Listening Tip

Be sure to wait until your partner has finished speaking before asking a question or adding new information.

# Let's Wrap Up!

**? Essential Question**

## How can being a good citizen make a difference to others?

· · · · · · · · · · · · · · · · · · · · · · · · · · · · · · · · · · · · · · · · · · · · · · · · · · · · · · · · · ·

**Pick one of these activities to show what you have learned about the topic.**

## 1. The Award Goes to...

You have read about what it means to be a good citizen. Think about someone you know who has made a difference to others. Compare the person to one of the characters you read about. Create a Super Citizen Certificate for that person. Tell a partner whom you chose and why.

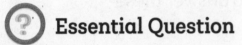

## 2. A Letter to Me

We can all make a difference in our own special way. How will YOU be a good citizen this year? Write a letter to yourself to explain your plan. Think about what you are good at and what you like to do. Look back at the texts for ideas about how to be a good citizen.

**Word Challenge**

Can you use the word difference in your letter?

## My Notes

# Look Around and Explore!

"Isn't it splendid to think of all the things there are to find out about?"

—L. M. Montgomery

Essential Question

# How does exploring help us understand the world around us?

Get Curious Video

# Words About Discovering Our World

Complete the Vocabulary Network to show what you know about the words.

## examine

**Meaning:** When you **examine** something, you look at it carefully.

| Synonyms and Antonyms | Drawing |
|---|---|
| | |

# identify

**Meaning:** When you **identify** something, you say what it is.

| Synonyms and Antonyms | Drawing |
|---|---|
| | |

# record

**Meaning:** When you **record** notes, you write them down.

| Synonyms and Antonyms | Drawing |
|---|---|
| | |

# What's the Matter?

Everything around you is made up of matter. There are three kinds of matter: **solid**, **liquid**, and **gas**.

Look around for different kinds of matter right in your classroom. Use the **Kinds of Matter** section to figure out what kind of matter each thing is. Can you find all three kinds of matter?

Which kind of matter did you find the most of?

# Kinds of Matter

**SOLID**
A solid's shape does not change.

**LIQUID**
A liquid becomes the shape of its container.

**GAS**
A gas does not have a shape. It fits all the space in its container.

Examples of Solids

Examples of Liquids

Examples of Gases

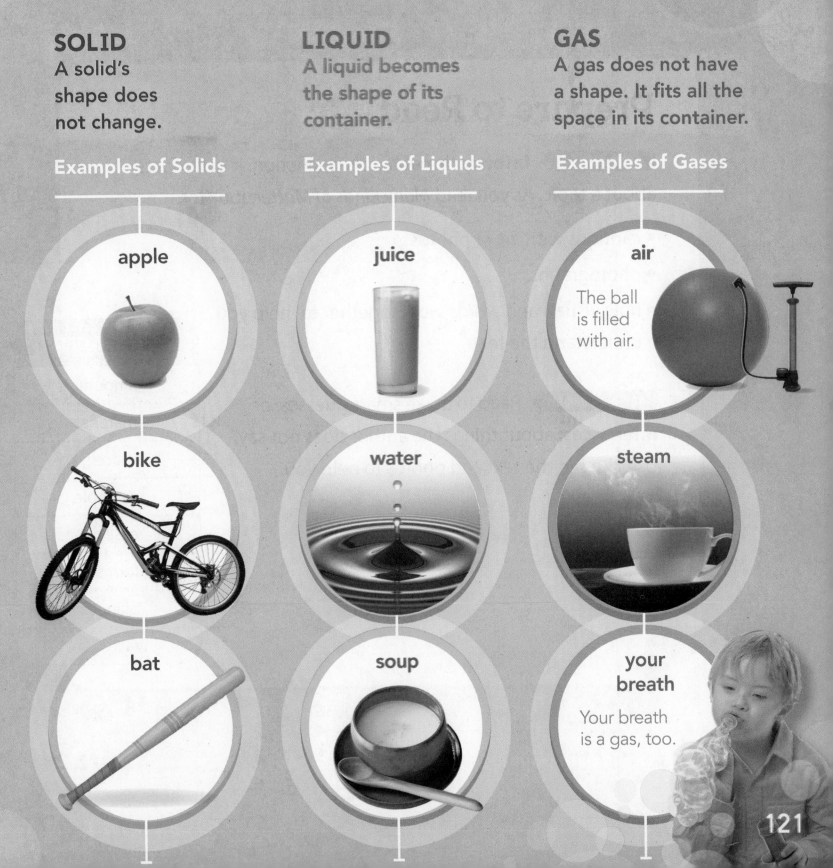

apple

juice

air

The ball is filled with air.

bike

water

steam

bat

soup

your breath

Your breath is a gas, too.

121

# Prepare to Read

**GENRE STUDY**  **Informational text** is nonfiction. It gives facts about a topic. As you read *Many Kinds of Matter*, look for:

- captions with art or photos
- photographs
- how visuals and words work together to help you understand the text

**SET A PURPOSE**  Read to make smart guesses, or **inferences,** about things the author does not say. Use clues in the text and photos to help you.

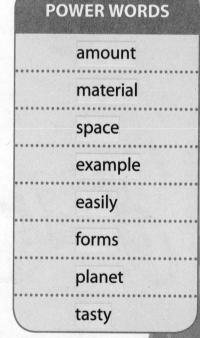

| POWER WORDS |
| --- |
| amount |
| material |
| space |
| example |
| easily |
| forms |
| planet |
| tasty |

**Build Background: Solids, Liquids, and Gases**

# MANY KINDS OF
# MATTER

by Jennifer Boothroyd

# MATTER

Matter is everywhere. Matter is anything that has mass and volume. Mass is the amount of material in an object. Volume is the amount of space an object takes up.

Trees, lakes, and people are matter. All have mass and volume.

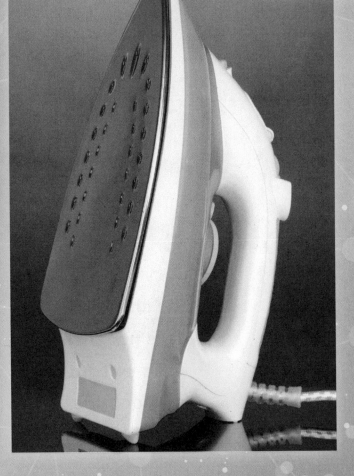

There are three
kinds of matter.

**The three
kinds of
matter are
solids, liquids,
and gases.**

# SOLIDS

## Books, rocks, and toys are solids.

Solid matter holds its own shape. Solids do not take the shape of their container. Marbles fill a jar. But the marbles are still round.

Books are one **example** of a solid.

The shape of solids does not change when you put them in a container.

Solids are not easy to compress. *Compress* means to squeeze something into a tight space. Bottles and cans are solids. It's not easy to squeeze them into this recycling bin!

Solids do not flow.
Solid candies don't spread
across ice cream the way
hot fudge sauce does.

Candy sprinkles
are solids. They
do not flow over
ice cream.

# LIQUIDS

**Oil, syrup, and water are liquids.**

Liquid matter does not hold its own shape. Liquids take the shape of their container. Water inside a swimming pool takes on the shape of the pool.

Oil is one example of a liquid.

Water in a square pool takes on a square shape.

Liquids are not easy to compress. Milk is a liquid. You couldn't fit the milk in the jug into the little carton.

Liquids flow. Liquid syrup spreads across pancakes.

# GASES

Air, steam, and your breath are gases.

Your breath is one example of a gas.

Gas matter does not hold its own shape. Gases take the shape of their container. The air inside a hot air balloon takes on the shape of the balloon.

Gases are easy to compress. Carbon dioxide is a gas. It's inside soda cans. It's squeezed into the cans to give the soda bubbles.

Carbon dioxide rushes out of soda cans when you open them.

Gases flow. The air inside a bubble spreads to fill the space inside the bubble.

# MATTER AND CHANGES

## Matter can change from one kind to another.

Some solids can change to liquids. Some liquids can change to gases.

Water is a special kind of matter. You know that water is a liquid. But it can easily be found in all three forms on our planet.

**The liquid in this cup is changing to a gas.**

Water becomes a solid if it is cooled.

## It turns into ice.

Water turns into ice when it freezes. Water freezes when it reaches a temperature of 32°F (0°C).

Water becomes a gas if it is heated.

## It turns into steam.

Water turns into steam when it boils. Water boils when it reaches a temperature of 212°F (100°C).

Water at any temperature can change into water vapor. Water vapor is a gas.

**This change is called evaporation.**

Some people use a drying rack after washing their dishes. The dishes dry after the water evaporates.

Water vapor changes back into liquid water when it cools in the air.

**This change is called condensation.**

You can see condensation after a hot shower. The water vapor touches the shower door and turns back into a liquid.

Have you ever seen condensation on a shower door?

Other matter can change forms, too. Cheese is a solid. It melts when it gets hot. It changes to a liquid.

Bread dipped in melted cheese is a **tasty** treat.

Juice is a liquid. It freezes when it gets cold. It changes to a solid.

Ice pops can be made by freezing juice.

# We use solids, liquids, and gases every day.

They are an important part of our lives and our planet.

Use details from *Many Kinds of Matter* to answer these questions with a partner.

1.  **Make Inferences** Look at the cup on page 134. What is causing the liquid in that cup to change to a gas? How do you know?

2.  Compare the three kinds of matter. How are solids, liquids, and gases the same? How are they different?

3.  What examples does the text give for each kind of matter? What other examples can you name?

## Listening Tip

Listen politely to your partner, and wait until it is your turn to speak.

# Write a Description

**PROMPT** How does a snowman change as it melts? Use details from the words and pictures in *Many Kinds of Matter* to explain your ideas.

**PLAN** First, picture a snowman in your mind and write words that describe it. Then, picture a melted snowman and write words that describe it.

| Snowman | Melted Snowman |
|---------|----------------|
|         |                |

**WRITE** Now, write sentences to describe how a snowman changes as it melts. Remember to:

- Find details in the text and pictures that tell about how matter can change.

- Use describing words.

_____

_____

_____

_____

_____

_____

_____

_____

_____

# Prepare to Read

**GENRE STUDY** **Informational text** is nonfiction. It gives facts about a topic.

**MAKE A PREDICTION** Preview "Are You Curious?" Our world is full of things that make us wonder and feel curious. What do you think you will read about?

_____

_____

_____

_____

_____

_____

**SET A PURPOSE** Read to make inferences about people who are curious.

# Are You Curious?

**READ** Which words help you understand what *curious* means? <u>Underline</u> them.

Being curious means wondering about things. It means being excited to explore. When we are curious, we ask questions. We might ask questions about how something works or why things happen. We can observe things we are curious about. This helps us find answers. Those answers can surprise us. They might even make us more curious! ▶

**Close Reading Tip**

Mark important ideas with a *.

## CHECK MY UNDERSTANDING

How do people find answers when they are curious?

_____

_____

_____

**READ** Which sentences help you understand how being curious can lead to making discoveries? <u>Underline</u> them.

**Close Reading Tip**

Circle words you don't know. Then figure them out. If you need to, look them up in a dictionary.

Curiosity leads to learning and new, exciting discoveries. Long ago, people asked, "Why can birds fly?" They watched birds in the sky. They discovered that a bird's wing shape was one reason why it could fly. Eventually, what people had learned about a bird's wings was used to build the airplane.

We know a lot about the world around us because people were curious. And there are always more questions we can ask! Never be afraid to say, "I don't know." That will help your curiosity grow. We can only learn what we don't know.

What do you wonder about?

**CHECK MY UNDERSTANDING**

What can you infer from the text about people who are curious?

_____

_____

_____

_____

146

**WRITE ABOUT IT**  What makes you a curious person? Use details from the text in your answer. Try to include the words *wonder*, *discovery*, and *curious*.

_____

_____

_____

_____

_____

_____

_____

_____

_____

_____

_____

**147**

# Prepare to Read

**GENRE STUDY** **Fantasies** are stories with made-up events that could not really happen. As you read *The Great Fuzz Frenzy,* look for:

- animal characters that talk and act like people
- the beginning, middle, and ending of the story
- setting, or where the story takes place

**SET A PURPOSE** As you read, **make connections** by finding ways that this text is like things in your life and other texts you have read. This will help you understand and remember the text.

### POWER WORDS

gasped

frenzy

battleground

feud

**Meet Janet Stevens and Susan Stevens Crummel.**

by Janet Stevens and Susan Stevens Crummel

illustrated by Janet Stevens

# THE GREAT FUZZ FRENZY

"Violet! No!"

"Violet! Where's the ball?"

"WOOF!"

150

151

# PLUNK.

There it sat—perfectly still.
The prairie dogs waited—perfectly still.

Slowly they crept out.

Inch by inch. Dog by dog.

"What is it?"

"A thing."

"A good thing or a bad thing?"

154

155

"Stand back!" boomed a voice. "You act like gutless groundhogs—afraid of your own shadow!"

"Oh no, it's Big Bark!"

"Big *Mouth* is more like it."

"He's the meanest dog around."

"I thought he left town."

"Well, I'm back," growled Big Bark. "So out of my way. Let me have a look."

But before anyone could move, little Pip Squeak raced past Big Bark, reached out, and poked the big round thing.

"Noooooo!" the crowd yelled.

"It's fuzzy!" said Pip.

"Oooooooh!" the crowd gasped.

A tiny piece of fuzz was caught in Pip's claw. She looked at it. Turned it. Sniffed it. Then she put it on her head. "Look at me!"

"Ahhhhhh!" the crowd sighed.

"Quit hammin' it up, you half-pint hamster!" snarled Big Bark. *"I'm in charge."*

157

But those prairie dogs didn't listen. They had to have fuzz.

"I like it."

"Me, too."

"I want some."

"Do you?"

"Oh yes!"

"So do I!"

"So do we!"

"So do they!"

"Big Bark, move over!"

"Get out of our way!"

They charged past him
and grabbed at the fuzz.

The prairie dogs pulled it. Puffed it.
Stretched it. Fluffed it.
Tugged it. Twirled it.
Spiked it. Swirled it.
They fuzzed their ears, their heads, their noses.
They fuzzed their feet, their tails, their toeses.

Big Bark was beside himself. "Listen to me, you ridiculous rodents! Stop this fuzzy foolishness!"

But those prairie dogs didn't listen.
They were busy being hot dogs and silly dogs.
Corny dogs and frilly dogs.
Top dogs. Funny dogs.
Superdogs. Bunny dogs.

"You're all nuts, you squirrelly fuzz freaks!" yelled Big Bark, storming off.

News of the fuzz spread from hole to hole. Burrow to burrow. Town to town.

Soon prairie dogs from everywhere were coming to see that fuzz.

They came, they saw, they picked.

163

They twisted it. Braided it. Danced, and paraded it.
It was a fuzz frenzy.
A fuzz fiesta.
A fuzz fandangle.
The whole prairie was abuzz about fuzz.

They picked and pruned and pulled and pinched.
They pinched and pulled and pruned and picked.

Until . . .
the fuzz ran out.

That big round thing was fuzzless. Naked as a plucked chicken.

Some prairie dogs got a lot of fuzz.
Some got a little. Some got no fuzz
at all—and they were mad.

"Give me that fuzz!"
    "Why?"

"Because."
    "It's my fuzz."
        "Well, it *was!*"

"Get that fuzz!"

"GET THAT
FUZZ!"

Pulling, grabbing, swiping, nabbing, poking, jabbing—it was war! War between the fuzzes and the fuzz-nots. Their peaceful town was a **battleground**.

It was a fuzz fight.

A fuzz **feud**.

A fuzz fiasco.

"I started this," moaned Pip Squeak. "I have to do something. Everyone! Stop! Stop fighting!"

But those prairie dogs didn't listen. The battle raged
on—friend against friend, cousin against cousin, dog against
dog—until no one was left standing.

They were pooped. Fuzzled out. Fast asleep.

Hours later the prairie dogs began to stir.
"Uh-oh!"
"Where's the fuzz?"
"I don't know!"
"Where did it go?"
"SOMEONE HAS STOLEN OUR FUZZ!"
cried Pip Squeak.

"I DID!" barked a voice from above.

"I STOLE THE FUZZ!"

The prairie dogs froze. Then they raced up, up, up the long tunnel. There stood Big Bark, covered with fuzz from head to tail.

"I'm king of the fuzz!" he snarled. "Do you hear me? I'm king of the—"

# SWOOP!

**The sky went black.**

"What happened?"

"Where's Big Bark?"

"Look!"

There he was, high above their heads, dangling from the talons of an eagle.

"No more Big Bark!" the crowd cheered. "Yaaaaaay!"

"Don't *yaaaaaay*! He's one of *us*!" yelled Pip. "We have to save him! How would *you* like to be Eagle's lunch?"

"Noooooo!" the crowd yelled.

"Big Bark, wiggle free!" the prairie dogs shouted.

"Shake loose!"

"Hurry!"

"We"ll catch you!"

Big Bark twisted and turned, wormed and squirmed. At last he was free of the fuzz!

"Yaaaaaay!" the crowd cheered.

Big Bark fell faster and faster.
"Noooooo!" Prairie dogs scattered.

"Get back here!" yelled Pip. "Quick!
Make a circle! Hold out your paws!"
They ran left, then right, then left.

# PLOP!

"You saved me!" Big Bark cried. "But I stole your fuzz! Now it's gone forever."

"Good," said Pip Squeak. "Fuzz is *trouble*. Right?"

"Yaaaaaay!" the crowd cheered. Friend hugged friend. Cousin hugged cousin. Dog hugged dog.

"We don't need fuzz," said Pip. "But with Eagle around, we do need a watchdog with a big—"

"BAAARRRK!" Big Bark rose
up on his hind legs. "Eagle's back!
BAAARRRK! This is not a test!
BAAARRRK! All dogs below!
BAAARRRK!"

The prairie dogs raced down,
down, down the long tunnel.

179

"Whew! We made it!"

"That was close!"

"Three cheers for Big Bark, the best watchdog ever!"

"YIP, YIP, YAAAAAAY! YIP, YIP, YAAAAAAY! YIP, YIP, YAAAAAAY!"

"Just doing my job!" Big Bark smiled.

"Are we ever getting tangled up with fuzz again?" cried Pip Squeak.

"Noooooo!" the crowd yelled. "No more fuzz! No more fuzz!"

And from that day forward, the prairie dogs lived happily—and
fuzzlessly—ever after.

Use details from *The Great Fuzz Frenzy* to answer these questions with a partner.

1. **Make Connections** Think about a time when it was hard for you to share. How does that help you understand what happens when the prairie dogs find the fuzz?

2. Why do the prairie dogs cheer when Eagle takes Big Bark? Why do their feelings change?

3. Find places in the story where the authors repeat words and sounds. How does this make the story fun to read?

## Talking Tip

Ask to learn more about one of your partner's ideas. Complete the sentence below.

Tell me more about _____.

# Write an Invitation

**PROMPT** The prairie dogs have a celebration after they find the tennis ball. What could they say to persuade other prairie dogs to join in the fun? Use details from the words and pictures to explain your ideas.

**PLAN** First, think of reasons why other prairie dogs would want to join the celebration. Write or draw them below.

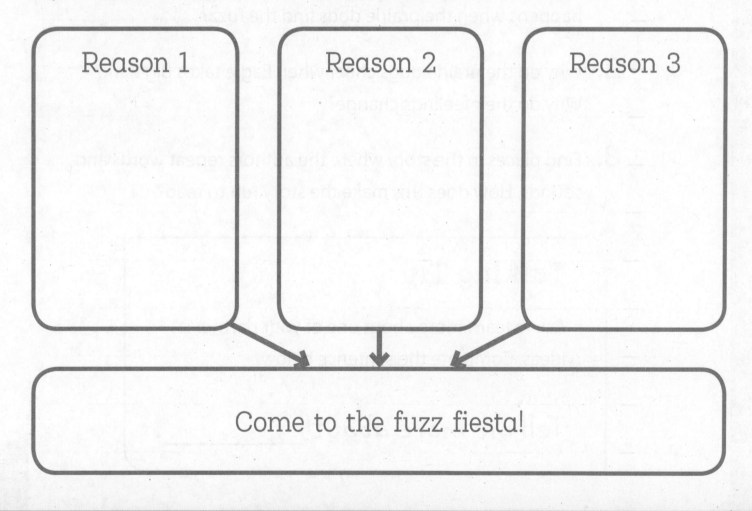

| Reason 1 | Reason 2 | Reason 3 |
| --- | --- | --- |
| | | |

Come to the fuzz fiesta!

**WRITE** Now, write sentences to invite the prairie dogs to the fuzz fiesta. Remember to:

- Look for details in the story that show how the prairie dogs feel about fuzz.

- Describe the celebration in a way that will make other prairie dogs excited about going.

_____

_____

_____

_____

_____

_____

_____

_____

_____

# Prepare to Read

**GENRE STUDY** **Fantasies** are stories with made-up events that could not really happen.

**MAKE A PREDICTION** Preview "Bear Up There." Grandpa, Billie Bear, and Honeysuckle are lost in the woods. You know that a fantasy has make-believe events. What do you think will happen?

_____

_____

_____

_____

_____

_____

_____

**SET A PURPOSE** Read to find out what happens to the bears when it gets dark outside.

# Bear Up There

**READ** How would you feel if you were Billie?

"Grandpa, we're lost!" Billie Bear's cry cut through the Great Wood. Her twin, Honeysuckle, opened her eyes wide.

The cubs loved hiking with Grandpa. He never told them to hurry. He liked to move slowly. Today they had picked lots of blueberries. They had splashed in a river and fished for salmon. Now it was getting dark, and they were lost. ▶

**Close Reading Tip**

Write C when you make a connection.

## CHECK MY UNDERSTANDING

How does the illustration help you understand what Grandpa is like?

_____

_____

_____

185

**READ** Make connections to times in your life when you learned something new that helped you.

**Close Reading Tip**

What prediction did you make about the events you would read in this fantasy? What were you right about? What was different?

"A bear is never lost," Grandpa said with a wink. "The Great Bear will take us home." Grandpa's paw traced the outline of a huge bear in the stars. "That bear up there is Ursa Major. *Ursa* means bear, and *major* means big."

"There IS a bear up there!" Honeysuckle cried out.

"There are four paws!" Billie pointed. "I see a nose, too. But how…?"

"The first paw points to our den," Grandpa said.

Billie Bear and Honeysuckle jumped for joy.

"Grandpa is so wise," Honeysuckle said. "I can't wait to tell Mama what he showed us!"

**CHECK MY UNDERSTANDING**

How does Grandpa solve the problem in the story?

_____

_____

_____

**WRITE ABOUT IT**  Write what happens next! Use details from the story to write what Billie and Honeysuckle tell their mother when they get home. Draw a picture to go with your writing.

_____

_____

_____

_____

_____

_____

_____

_____

_____

_____

# Prepare to Read

**GENRE STUDY** **Poetry** uses images, sounds, and rhythm to express feelings. As you read *Water Rolls, Water Rises*, look for:

- alliteration, or a pattern of words with the same first sound (like *can* and *cats*)
- the line breaks in each stanza
- repetition of sounds, words, or lines
- words that appeal to the senses

**SET A PURPOSE** As you read, use the poet's words to **create mental images,** or make pictures in your mind. How do the pictures help you understand what the poet is describing?

**POWER WORDS**

strokes

tumbling

plumes

wisps

**Meet Pat Mora.**

# Water Rolls, Water Rises

by Pat Mora   illustrated by Meilo So

*W*ater rolls
onto the shore
under the sun, under the moon.

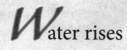

*W*ater rises
into soft fog,
weaves down the street, strokes an old cat.

192

Blown by the wind,
water sails high.
Tumbling cloud plumes curl through the air.

Slow into rivers,
water slithers and snakes
through silent canyons at twilight and dawn.

Down smooth canals,
water streams, water slides,
gliding up roots of tulips and corn.

Filling deep wells,
water hums in the dark,
sloshes in buckets, quenches our thirst.

*S*wirling in wisps,
water twists then it twirls,
frosts scattered dry leaves, rubs lonely, bare trees.

*I*n storms, water plunges
in thunder's brash roar,
races through branches from lightning's white flash.

Then water rests,
drowsy in reservoirs,
its glistening silence shimmers like stars.

In the murmur of marsh wind,
water slumbers on moss,
whispers soft songs far under frog feet.

Water burbles in springs,
gurgles and turns
down streams and rivers seeking the sea.

$S$kidding and slipping,
swooping round bends,
spinning on tree roots, careening down cliffs.

Looping and leaping,
rushing to dive
into glimmering sea waves, spangle and splash.

Around our round world,
water rolls, water rises
under gold sun, under white moon.

Use details from *Water Rolls, Water Rises* to answer these questions with a partner.

1. **Create Mental Images** Close your eyes and picture one of the settings in the text. Describe what you see, hear, and smell. Which of the author's words help you create the picture?

2. Why do you think the author wrote this text? What does she want readers to know?

3. Why do you think this text uses illustrations instead of photographs to picture the author's words?

## Talking Tip

Ask to learn more about one of your partner's ideas. Complete the sentence below.

Please explain _____.

# Write a Poem

**PROMPT**  How would you describe water in a poem? Find important details in the words and pictures from *Water Rolls, Water Rises* to help you explain your ideas.

**PLAN**  First, make a details chart. On one side, write details about water. Then, think of interesting words that describe each detail. Write them on the other side of your chart.

| Details | Words |
| --- | --- |
|  |  |

**WRITE** Now write your poem using the best words from the chart. Remember to:

- Use words that paint a picture of your topic.
- Think about how the words in your poem sound together.

_____

_____

_____

_____

_____

_____

_____

_____

_____

# Prepare to Read

**GENRE STUDY** **Poetry** uses images, sounds, and rhythm to express feelings.

**MAKE A PREDICTION** Preview "Matter Matters." What feelings might these two poems express? What might they be about?

_____

_____

_____

_____

_____

_____

_____

**SET A PURPOSE** Read to see how poetry uses words in a special way to share information.

# Matter Matters

**READ** In each line of the poem, look for words that begin with the same letter. <u>Underline</u> those words.

**S**ome can be big, bumpy, or boxy.

**O**thers can be small, sparkly, or squishy.

**L**et me give you a hint.

**I**t is the kind of matter that

**D**oes not change its

**S**hape! ▶

> **Close Reading Tip**
>
> Put a **?** by the parts you have questions about.

## CHECK MY UNDERSTANDING

Why did the poet make the first letter of each line bold?

_____

_____

_____

**READ** Which of the poet's words help you to create a picture in your mind? <u>Underline</u> those words.

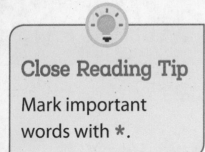

**Close Reading Tip**

Mark important words with *.

**L**iquids are everywhere,

**I**n splashing seas and tiny teacups.

**Q**uiet streams slowly slide,

**U**nless they freeze and turn to

**I**ce.

**D**on't slip!

**CHECK MY UNDERSTANDING**

What do you learn about matter from this poem? Use your own words to describe the poet's ideas.

_____

_____

_____

_____

_____

**WRITE ABOUT IT** Write a poem like the poems in "Matter Matters." First, choose a state of matter. Write *SOLID, LIQUID,* or *GAS* in capital letters down the side of the paper. Next, write a sentence or phrase that begins with that letter on each line. What will your poem tell readers about that kind of matter?

_____

_____

_____

_____

_____

_____

_____

_____

_____

_____

# Prepare to Read

**GENRE STUDY** **Dramas** are plays that are read and performed. As you read *The Puddle Puzzle*, pay attention to:

- the cast of characters
- dialogue, or what the characters say
- setting, or where and when the story takes place
- stage directions that tell performers what to do

**SET A PURPOSE** **Ask questions** before, during, and after you read to help you get information or understand the text. Look for evidence in the text and pictures to **answer** your questions.

**POWER WORDS**

agency

business

confidently

eagerly

seeps

mystery

ace

located

**Meet Ellen Weiss.**

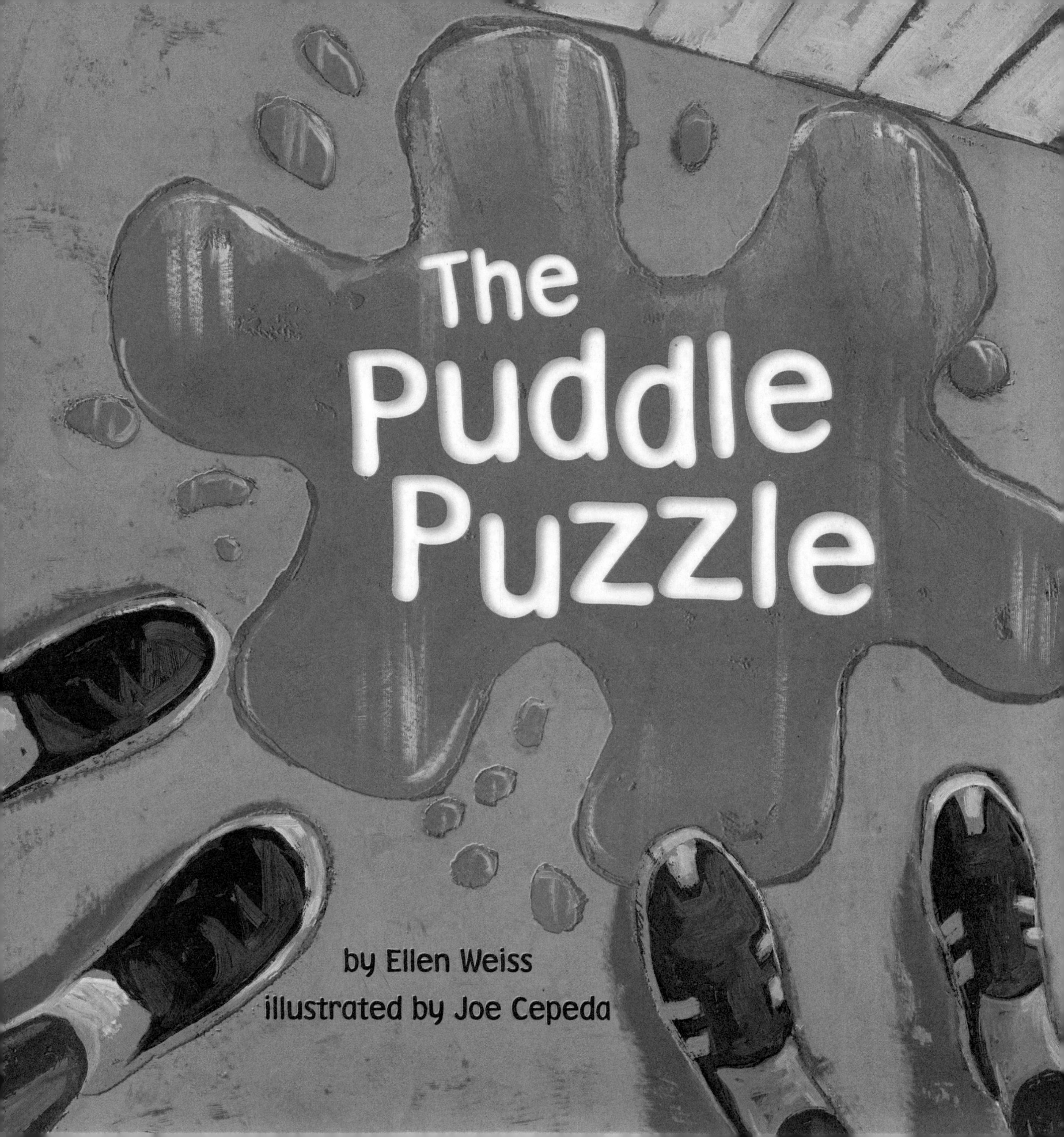

# The Puddle Puzzle

by Ellen Weiss

illustrated by Joe Cepeda

**Cast of Characters**

TAYLOR

BRANDON

CARLOS

ADRIANA

**Setting**

a neighborhood on
a sunny spring day

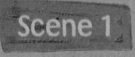

**Scene 1**

**TAYLOR:** I am so excited! The Miller Detective Agency is open for business!

**BRANDON:** I am excited, too!

**TAYLOR:** Now we just have to wait for our first customer.

**CARLOS:** Is that the detective agency?

**TAYLOR:** Come over! We are open!

**CARLOS:** I am Carlos, and this is my sister Adriana. We have a problem.

**TAYLOR:** We are here to help! What is your problem?

**CARLOS:** Our puddle has vanished.

**ADRIANA:** We were playing in the puddle. Then the sun went away, so we went inside for lunch. When the sun came back out, we went outside to play again.

Miller

**CARLOS:** But our puddle was gone! Can you help us find it?

**TAYLOR:** This is a very hard case. We will do our best to solve it for you.

**BRANDON:** *(smiling confidently)* I know the answer! I know!

**TAYLOR:** Shhh, Brandon. I am the oldest, so I am in charge. We need to go and look for clues.

**TAYLOR:** This is where your puddle was located?

**CARLOS:** Yes, it was right here.

**TAYLOR:** *(taking out her notebook and writing)* One puddle, missing. *(She looks around.)* Maybe somebody stole it. Was anyone around here?

**CARLOS:** Nobody!

**TAYLOR:** Maybe it is hiding. I will look behind this bush. Nope! It is not here.

**BRANDON:** *(eagerly)* I know what happened!

**TAYLOR:** Shhh, Brandon!

**BRANDON:** But I know what happened!

**TAYLOR:** Now I am looking for footprints.

**ADRIANA:** Maybe we should let Brandon talk.

**BRANDON:** Thank you! Ahem. *(He clears his throat.)* A puddle is full of water, right?

**CARLOS:** Right!

**BRANDON:** But water can have three different forms.

**CARLOS:** It can?

**BRANDON:** Yes! When we are splashing in a puddle, the water is a liquid. If you freeze water, it turns into a solid.

**ADRIANA:** Ice!

**BRANDON:** There is one more thing water can be, too. It can be a gas.

**ADRIANA:** A gas?

**BRANDON:** Yes! When we boil water, the steam that seeps out of the kettle is a gas. When the sun shines on a puddle and heats it up, the water turns into a gas, too. A gas does not have a shape or a size. Sometimes we cannot even see it!

**CARLOS:** So that is what happened to our puddle!

**BRANDON:** It went into the air, and now we cannot see it or feel it. This is called evaporation.

**TAYLOR:** Mystery solved!

**TAYLOR:** Brandon, I'm sorry I didn't let you talk today. You knew the answer and I was too excited about gathering clues to listen. I think we need a new sign.

**BRANDON:** *(smiling proudly)* That is much better.

**TAYLOR:** We are ace detectives!

Miller & Miller
Science Detective
Agency

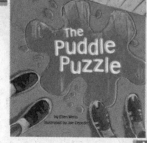

Use details from *The Puddle Puzzle* to answer these questions with a partner.

1. **Ask and Answer Questions** What questions did you ask yourself as Brandon and Taylor tried to solve the mystery? What questions did you ask at the end?

2. Which details explain what happened to the missing puddle?

3. How does the new sign make Brandon feel at the end of the drama? Why does he feel that way?

## Talking Tip

Complete the sentence to add more to one of your partner's answers.

I'd like to add that _____.

# Write Stage Directions

**PROMPT** Where would you add more stage directions to help readers perform the drama? Use details from the words and pictures to explain your answer.

**PLAN** First, draw a scene from the drama. Add labels that tell what the characters are doing or feeling.

**WRITE** Now write stage directions you would like to add to the drama. Be sure they describe what the characters are doing or feeling as they say their lines. Remember to:

- Include words that clearly describe actions or feelings.

- Include the character's lines that the stage directions go with. Think about how you would read them.

_____

_____

_____

_____

_____

_____

_____

_____

_____

# Prepare to Read

**Dramas** are stories that are read and performed.

Preview "Disappearing Daisies." Brandon and Taylor have a brand new case to solve. You know that dramas have characters, dialogue, and a setting. What do you think this drama will be about?

_____

_____

_____

_____

_____

_____

Read to solve the case before Brandon and Taylor. As you read, ask yourself, "Is this an important clue?"

# Disappearing Daisies

**READ** <u>Underline</u> the setting. Why is the setting important?

> **Cast of Characters:** Brandon, Mom, Narrator, Taylor
> **Setting:** the Miller home

MOM: I have a mystery to solve, kids. I need your help.

TAYLOR: Tell us the facts, and don't leave anything out.

MOM: Some daisies are missing from my flower garden. There are footprints all around the garden that are not mine.

NARRATOR: Brandon and Taylor looked at each other.

BRANDON: (*thoughtfully*) This is an interesting case. I think we can help.

TAYLOR: Yes, let's go dig up some clues in the flower garden. ▶

**Close Reading Tip**

Put a **?** by the parts you have questions about.

**Close Reading Tip**

Put a ! by a surprising part.

**READ** Look for a clue to help solve the mystery. <u>Underline</u> it.

NARRATOR: They went to the backyard to investigate.

BRANDON: When did you notice the flowers were missing?

MOM: Just a few minutes ago. They were here yesterday.

BRANDON: And is there anything special about this date?

TAYLOR: Yes, it's June 25th. Does that date mean anything to you?

MOM: *(looking surprised)* It's my birthday! I forgot all about it.

NARRATOR: Brandon and Taylor grinned. Brandon held out a big bouquet of daisies.

BRANDON and TAYLOR: Happy Birthday, Mom! We picked these for you!

MOM: You kids are the best detectives ever!

TAYLOR: Another case closed. Now, let's celebrate!

---

**CHECK MY UNDERSTANDING**

What questions did you ask yourself as you were trying to solve the mystery of the missing daisies?

_____

_____

**WRITE ABOUT IT** You used what you know about the characters, dialogue, and setting to help you make predictions. Did your predictions match what happened in the drama? Write to tell what you were right about. Tell what happened differently.

_____

_____

_____

_____

_____

_____

_____

_____

_____

_____

# Prepare to Read

**GENRE STUDY** **Fine art** describes art such as paintings, drawings, music, and dance. As you read *Looking at Art*, notice:

- people or objects in the art
- how the art makes you feel
- the subject of the art
- the type of artwork

**SET A PURPOSE** Look at what is happening in the art. Think about how it creates a story in your mind. Compare what you see in the art to what you read in the text.

**Build Background: Art Critics**

# LOOKING AT ART

by Andrew Stevens

How does art imitate life? You learn things about the world around you every day. How can you do that with a painting? You can look at art for clues to help you understand what you see.

Jean Siméon Chardin painted *Soap Bubbles* around the year 1733. It shows a boy blowing a bubble. See his cheeks? If he were using big breaths, his cheeks would be puffed out. He must know the bubble will pop if it grows too quickly! The boy might be hoping the air will carry the bubble away.

If you lived in France long ago, you might see this scene in your neighborhood. What else can you figure out by studying the painting?

**Jean Siméon Chardin,**
***Soap Bubbles***
**oil on canvas**

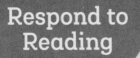 

Use details from *Looking at Art* and the painting *Soap Bubbles* to answer these questions with a partner.

**1.** **Connect Text and Visuals** What details from the image or the text tell you the painting was made a long time ago? How would it look different if the artist painted it today?

**2.** What are the characters doing in the painting? What do you think they will do next?

**3.** How does the author use words about science to tell about the painting?

## Listening Tip

You learn from others by listening carefully. Think about what your partner says and what you learn.

# Let's Wrap Up!

**? Essential Question**

## How does exploring help us understand the world around us?

**Pick one of these activities to show what you have learned about the topic.**

**Word Challenge**

Can you use the word examine in your tips?

**1.** 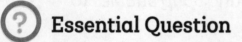 **Observe, Explore, Discover!**

You have read about how observing can help you learn about our world. Write five tips to help someone explore and make new discoveries. Look back at the texts for ideas about places and ways to explore.

bouncy

round

## 2. Picture the Matter

Draw or find pictures for each of
the different kinds of matter. Then
make a collage. Add labels to describe
how the objects in your collage look, sound,
feel, smell, or taste.

## My Notes

# Glossary

## A

**ace** [ās]   Someone described as **ace** is extremely good at something.

He is an **ace** soccer player.

**agency** [ā′jən-sē]   If you work at an **agency**, your job is to help others to get something done.

My neighbor works for a health **agency**.

**amount** [ə-mount′]   An **amount** is how much there is of something.

I would like a small **amount** of juice.

## B

**battleground** [băt′l-ground′]   A **battleground** is where a fight takes place.

I visited the **battleground** where the war was won many years ago.

ace

amount

**bellowed** [bĕl′ōd]   If you **bellowed**, you shouted in a loud, deep voice.

"Get away from there!" she **bellowed**.

**blue** [blōō]   When you feel **blue**, you feel sad.

We are feeling **blue** today.

**bounce** [bouns]   When you **bounce**, you move up and down.

I like to **bounce** my ball outside.

**business** [bĭz′nĭs]   A place open for **business** is ready to work, buy, or sell something.

The coffee shop is now open for **business**.

business

# C

**citizen** [sĭt′ĭ-zən]   A **citizen** is a member of a community, state, or country.

I am a **citizen** of the United States.

citizen

239

**compliment** [kŏm′plə-mənt]   A **compliment** is a nice thing to say about someone.
My teacher gave me a **compliment** about my work at school today.

**confidently** [kŏn′fĭ-dənt-lē]   When you do something **confidently**, you are sure you will do it well.
She spoke **confidently** to the crowd.

**cool** [kōōl]   To **cool** how you feel means to calm down.
Taking deep breaths helps me to **cool** down.

cool

# D

**difference** [dĭf′ər-əns, dĭf′rəns]   When people make a **difference**, they do something that helps others.
Picking up litter helps us make a **difference** in the community.

**disaster** [dĭ-zăs′tər, dĭ-săs′tər]   A **disaster** is an event that goes horribly wrong.
Leaving our dog alone with the new couch was a **disaster**, but we still love her.

disaster

# E

**eagerly** [ē′gər-lē]   When you do something **eagerly**, you really want to do it.
The student **eagerly** accepted her award.

**easily** [ē′zə-lē]   Something that is done **easily** is not hard to do.
You can win the race **easily**.

**elected** [ĭ-lĕkt′ĭd]   Someone who is **elected** has been chosen for a job.
My friend was **elected** to be class president.

elected

**examine** [ĭg-zăm′ĭn]   When you **examine** something, you look at it carefully.
We went outside to **examine** the footprints in the yard.

**example** [ĭg-zăm′pəl]   An **example** is a part of a larger group of things that are alike.
This beautiful painting is one **example** of my favorite artist's work.

examine

241

# F

feud

**feud** [fyo͞od]   A **feud** is a long fight.
My brother and I had a **feud** about sharing our toys.

**fiddled** [fĭd′ld]   If you **fiddled** with something, you kept touching it or playing with it.
The girl **fiddled** with the zipper on her jacket.

**forms** [fôrmz]   Something with many **forms** has different shapes or ways of being.
We are learning about the different **forms** of water in school today.

**frenzy** [frĕn′zē]   A **frenzy** is a time of great excitement and wild behavior.
The big sale caused a shopping **frenzy**.

# G

**gasped** [găspt]   If people **gasped**, they took a sharp breath in a surprised way.
We **gasped** with surprise at the most exciting part.

gasped

**grinned** [grĭnd]   If you **grinned**, you smiled a wide smile.

I **grinned** when I heard the happy news.

# H

**hamper** [hăm′pər]   A **hamper** is a basket with a lid, used to hold dirty clothes.

Please put your dirty clothes in the **hamper**.

**handle** [hăn′dl]   When you cannot **handle** something, you are not able to deal with it.

I can **handle** doing more chores if I have some help.

# I

**identify** [ĭ-dĕn′tə-fī′]   When you **identify** something, you say what it is.

I want to **identify** the type of insect we found.

grinned

hamper

**kind**

# K

**kind** [kīnd]   Someone who is **kind** is nice, caring, or gentle.

Helping others is one way to be **kind**.

# L

**local** [lō′kəl]   Something that is **local** belongs to the area where you live.

My mother works for the **local** newspaper.

**located** [lō′kāt′ĭd, lō-kāt′ĭd]   Where something is **located** is where it is.

The map shows where the ponds are **located**.

**located**

# M

**material** [mə-tîr′ē-əl]   **Material** is what something is made from.

What **material** is that shirt made out of?

**might** [mīt]   Doing something with all your **might** is using all your power.

He threw the ball with all his **might**.

**mock** [mŏk]   A **mock** version of something is not real.

We set up a **mock** doctor's office for toys.

**mood** [mo͞od]   Your **mood** is the way you are feeling.

I am in a great **mood** when I hear my favorite song.

**munch** [mŭnch]   When you **munch** food, you chew it loudly and completely.

My friend likes to **munch** on carrots.

**mystery** [mĭs′tə-rē]   A **mystery** is something that is hard to understand or is not known about.

The clues helped the detectives solve the **mystery**.

# P

**perfect** [pûr′fĭkt]   When something is **perfect**, it is the best it can be.

I felt proud of my **perfect** score on the quiz.

mock

mood

245

**planet**

**proper**

**planet** [plăn′ĭt]   A **planet** is a large object in space that moves around a star.
Earth is the third **planet** from the sun.

**planned** [plănd]   If you **planned**, you decided ahead of time how you would do something.
She **planned** to do her homework tomorrow.

**plumes** [ploōmz]   **Plumes** are long, thin shapes that look like feathers.
He saw **plumes** of smoke in the air.

**proper** [prŏp′ər]   Someone who is **proper** is polite and behaves well.
It is **proper** to use your best manners at a tea party.

# Q

**queasy** [kwē′zē]   If you are **queasy**, your stomach hurts and you feel sick.
She knew she would feel **queasy** if she ate too much popcorn, so she just had a little bit.

246

# R

**realize** [rē'ə-līz']   When you **realize** something, you know it or understand it.

Do you **realize** that the event ends in an hour?

**record** [rĭ-kôrd']   When you **record** notes, you write them down.

I like to **record** my story ideas in a notebook.

**rough** [rŭf]   When you do something in a **rough** way, you are not being gentle.

Some sports can be too **rough** for children.

record

# S

**scowl** [skoul]   A **scowl** is an angry frown.

She had a **scowl** on her face after she heard the game was canceled.

**seeps** [sēps]   When something **seeps**, it passes slowly through a small opening.

Honey **seeps** through a crack in the jar.

scowl

247

**space** [spās]   **Space** is an open area or place.
The pool takes up a large **space** in the yard.

**strokes** [strōks]   When something **strokes** something
else, it moves gently over that thing.
My dog likes when my friend **strokes** her fur.

**strokes**

# T

**tasty** [tā'stē]   Something that is **tasty** is good to eat.
This salad dressing is so **tasty**.

**tumbling** [tŭm'blĭng]   Something that is **tumbling** is
rolling over and over.
We had fun **tumbling** across the lawn.

**tumbling**

# U

**useful** [yoōs'fəl]   Something that is **useful**
is helpful.
The book has many **useful** tips about camping.

# W

**wisps** [wĭsps]   **Wisps** are thin streaks of something.
I saw **wisps** of clouds in the sky.

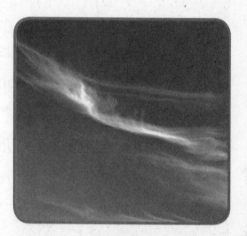

**wisps**

# Index of Titles and Authors

# Acknowledgments

Excerpt from *Being a Good Citizen* (retitled from *Being a Good Citizen: A Kids' Guide to Community Involvement*) by Rachelle Kreisman, illustrated by Tim Haggerty. Copyright © 2016 by Red Chair Press LLC. Reprinted with the permission of Red Chair Press LLC.

*Clark the Shark* by Bruce Hale, illustrated by Guy Francis. Text copyright © 2013 by Bruce Hale. Illustrations copyright © 2013 by Guy Francis. Reprinted by permission of HarperCollins Publishers.

*The Great Fuzz Frenzy* by Janet Stevens and Susan Stevens Crummel. Text copyright © 2005 by Janet Stevens and Susan Stevens Crummel. Illustrations copyright © 2005 by Janet Stevens. Reprinted by permission of Houghton Mifflin Harcourt Publishing Company.

Excerpt from *Many Kinds of Matter* (retitled from *Many Kinds of Matter: A Look at Solids, Liquids, and Gases*) by Jennifer Boothroyd. Text copyright © 2011 by Lerner Publishing Group, Inc. Reprinted with the permission of Lerner Publishing Company, a division of Lerner Publishing Group, Inc.

*Picture Day Perfection* by Deborah Diesen, illustrated by Dan Santat. Text copyright © 2013 by Deborah Diesen. Illustrations copyright © 2013 by Dan Santat. Reprinted by permission of Express Permissions on behalf of Abrams Books for Young Readers, an imprint of Harry N. Abrams, Inc., New York and Trident Media Group, LLC.

Excerpt by Christopher Reeve from http://www.spinalcordinjury-paralysis.org/blogs/16/1784. Text copyright © by Christopher Reeve. Reprinted by permission of the Estate of Christopher Reeve.

*Spoon* by Amy Krouse Rosenthal, illustrated by Scott Magoon. Text copyright © 2009 by Amy Krouse Rosenthal. Illustrations copyright © 2009 by Scott Magoon. Reprinted by permission of Hyperion Books for Children, an imprint of Disney Publishing Group.

*Water Rolls, Water Rises/El agua rueda, el agua sube* by Pat Mora, illustrated by Meilo So. Text copyright © 2014 by Pat Mora. Illustrations copyright © 2014 by Meilo So. Reprinted by permission of Children's Book Press, an imprint of Lee & Low Books Inc.

# Credits

4 (all) ©ESB Professional/Shutterstock; 5 (t) ©Jani Bryson/Studio J, Inc.; 5 (b) ©Houghton Mifflin Harcourt; 5 ©Houghton Mifflin Harcourt; 6 (t) ©Serhiy Kobyakov/Alamy; 6 (b) ©Elena Elisseeva/Dreamstime; 6 (b) ©Hasan Can Balcioglu/Dreamstime; 6 (b) ©Vlue/Dreamstime; 7 (b) ©Fuse/Corbis/Getty Images; 8 (c) ©Rawpixel/iStock/Getty Images Plus; 8 (bg) ©paulista/Shutterstock; 8 (l) ©Hero Images/Getty Images; 8 (r) ©DenKuvaiev/iStock/Getty Images Plus; 9 (r) ©PeopleImages/iStock/Getty Images Plus; 9 (l) ©JGalione/iStock/Getty Images Plus; 12 (l) ©jannoon028/Shutterstock; 13 (tl) ©MachineHeadz/iStock/Getty Images Plus/Getty Images; 13 (bl) ©monkeybusinessimages/iStock/Getty Images Plus; 13 (br) ©iofoto/iStock/Getty Images Plus/Getty Images; 13 (bc) ©LovArt/Shutterstock; 13 (tr) ©jannoon028/Shutterstock; 14 ©Sonya Sones; 66 ©wavebreakmedia/Shutterstock; 67 ©Jani Bryson/Studio J, Inc.; 68 ©J Horrocks/E+/Getty Images; 69 ©2xSamara.com/Shutterstock; 70 ©Monkey Business images/Shutterstock; 71 (r) ©asiseeit/iStockPhoto.com; 71 (l) ©Tomasz Trojanowski/Shutterstock; 71 (c) ©ForsterForest/iStock/Getty Images Plus; 72 ©Lisa F Young/Shutterstock; 73 ©Michele and Tom Grimm/Alamy; 74 ©Tomasz Markowski/Shutterstock; 75 (r) ©Nolte Lourens/Shutterstock; 75 (l) ©Robert Kneschke/Shutterstock; 76 ©Sergey Novikov/Shutterstock; 77 (tr) ©Jani Bryson/Studio J, Inc.; 79 (tr) ©Jani Bryson/Studio J, Inc.; 84 ©Abrams Books; 110 ©Houghton Mifflin Harcourt; 110 ©Houghton Mifflin Harcourt; 110 (bl) ©Olga1818/Shutterstock; 112 ©Houghton Mifflin Harcourt; 113 (tr) ©Houghton Mifflin Harcourt; 113 (tr) ©Houghton Mifflin Harcourt; 114 (tl) ©SolStock/iStock/Getty Images Plus/Getty Images; 114 (tr) ©glenda/Shutterstock; 114 (bl) ©pk74/iStock/Getty Images Plus; 114 (bc) ©skdesigns/iStock/Getty Images Plus; 115 ©Narvikk/E+/Getty Images; 116 ©gloriasalgado/RooM the Agency/Alamy; 120 ©Serhiy Kobyakov/Alamy; 121 (tl) ©MO_SES Premium/Shutterstock; 121 (cl) ©BillionPhotos.com/Fotolia; 121 (bl) ©amstockphoto/Shutterstock; 121 (tc) ©Judith Collins/Alamy; 121 (c) ©L. Clarke/Corbis; 121 (bc) ©yukibockle/Shutterstock; 121 (tr) ©Kletr/Shutterstock; 121 (cr) ©Africa Studio/Shutterstock; 121 (br) ©EVAfotografie/iStock/Getty Images Plus/Getty Images; 122 (bl) ©TunedIn by Westend61/Shutterstock; 122 (br) ©Elena Elisseeva/Dreamstime, (c) ©Hasan Can Balcioglu/Dreamstime, (cl) ©Vlue/Dreamstime, (bg) ©ber1a/Shutterstock; 124 ©Rubberball/Getty Images; 124 (bg) ©ber1a/Shutterstock; 125 (r) ©Stephen Smith/The Image Bank/Getty Images; 125 (c) ©Jjustas/